M000098068

Back Roads of the Carolinas

Farmhouse north of Cottonville, Stanly County, North Carolina

Books by Earl Thollander

Back Roads of New England
Back Roads of Oregon
Back Roads of Washington
Back Roads of California
Back Roads of Texas
Back Roads of Arizona
Barns of California
Earl Thollander's Back Roads of
    California

Back Roads of the Carolinas
by Earl Thollander

Clarkson N. Potter, Inc./Publishers NEW YORK

DISTRIBUTED BY CROWN PUBLISHERS, INC.

to Henry and Marsha

Pinxter, South Carolina

Map Legend

- 5.6 distance in miles between dots
- → → → my route (which may be reversed should you so desire)
- × my sketching place
- ■ towns and cities
- special place
- church of particular interest
- △ mountain
- ▲ campground
- picnic grounds
- water boundaries
- going under freeway
- .... ferry
- bridge
- tunnel
- interstate highway
- U.S. highway
- ◇ North Carolina highway
- Rd 1100 back road numbers
- ② South Carolina secondary highway
- South Carolina primary highway
- o historical marker
- BYP bypass
- BUS business
- cemetery

note: back road numbers often change when county boundaries are crossed

Copyright © 1985 by Earl Thollander

All rights reserved. No part of this book may be reproduced or transmitted in any form or by any means, electronic or mechanical, including photocopying, recording, or by any information storage and retrieval system, without permission in writing from the publisher.

Published by Clarkson N. Potter, Inc., One Park Avenue, New York, New York 10016, and simultaneously in Canada by General Publishing Company Limited

CLARKSON N. POTTER, POTTER, and colophon are trademarks of Clarkson N. Potter, Inc.

Manufactured in the United States of America

Library of Congress Cataloging in Publication Data

Thollander, Earl.
Back roads of the Carolinas.
Includes index.
1. North Carolina—Description and travel—1981- —Guide-books. 2. South Carolina—Description and travel—1981- —Guide-books. 3. Automobiles—Road guides—North Carolina. 4. Automobiles—Road guides—South Carolina. I. Title.
F252.3.T49 1985 917.56'0443 84-18278
ISBN 0-517-55658-8
10 9 8 7 6 5 4 3 2 1
First Edition

Contents

Thanks to artist Joe Seney and son, Wes, for good company on many of these back roads.

Preface

Back Roads of the Carolinas is a nonhighway travel guide to out-of-the-way places.

Each of the book's six parts begins with a sectional map. These will help you locate the back roads on larger state maps that are available from chambers of commerce, automobile clubs, travel services, tourist bureaus, and gas stations.

Localized maps for all roads mentioned throughout the book will guide you on specific trips. Arrows trace my direction of travel, although routes can easily be reversed. The North Pole is toward the top of the page. Maps are not to scale because the roads are of varying lengths; however, the mileage notations will provide a sense of their distance. Your odometer will not measure distance exactly the same as mine, but the differences should not be too great.

County maps were essential to me in following the back roads. They can be obtained at nominal cost from the North Carolina Department of Transportation, P.O. Box 25201, Raleigh, North Carolina 27611, and from the South Carolina Department of Highways, Map Sales Division, P.O. Drawer 191, Columbia, South Carolina 29202.

Landscape along Road 1600, near Louisburg, Franklin County, North Carolina

7

Old Church Ruin, Stokes County, North Carolina

Foreword by Charles Kuralt

Interstate highways, a marvel of the age, make it possible to cross the country from coast to coast without seeing anything. From the fast lane of an Interstate, every place looks like every other place, and the hamburger you buy beside the exit ramp in Maryland tastes just like the one you buy in Colorado. Once, at a rest stop near Spokane, I met a New Jersey family on vacation. "Having a good time?" I asked. "We sure are," said the father of the family as he climbed back behind the wheel of the station wagon. "We made five hundred miles yesterday, and we ought to make six hundred today. We have to be home by Sunday!"

That's one way to see the country, but it's not Earl Thollander's way. Ten or twelve miles is a good day's trip for him, and if a pretty farm in the bend of a pretty river catches his eye, he might take out his sketch pad and make no miles at all that day. To him America means local history and charming folklore, the slant of light on hills and fields, the smell of new-mown hay, and the sound of a banjo tune. Seen from its rutted farm roads and meandering blacktop byways, the United States of America is a land of rich differences. Vermonters, say, are not a bit like Alabamans. They have different ways of farming, different ways of talking, different senses of humor. These are dissimilarities that arise mainly from the land. You have to go slow enough to notice the land if you're ever going to appreciate the people who live on it.

In my own fashion, for nearly twenty years now, I've tried to go slow enough. My sketchbook weighs a little more than Earl Thollander's; it is a recording machine hooked up to a television camera. But out there "On the Road" for CBS News, I have tried to be true to the Thollander dictum that the back roads are the best roads. They are the ones that reveal a country's nature, yield up sudden delights, and leave you feeling satisfied. I have steered down many a back road with Mr. Thollander's maps and drawings on the seat beside me as guide and inspiration.

I have wondered when he was going to get around to the back roads of my own native region for I am, as we say down home, "a Tar Heel born and a Tar Heel bred, and when I die, I'm a Tar Heel dead!" Now that he's done it, slowly, in Thollander fashion, I find much in his pages of happy memory. These country roads of the Carolinas are the ones I know best of all. My grandmother's house stood beside one of Thollander's roads to New Bern. A well-loved cousin of mine lives on the road he followed down the New River (Oh, wonderful name for what may be the oldest river on the continent!), and as a boy, I rode my bicycle along the roads he describes around Pineville and Waxhaw. I am glad to know that these passages of my youth are still there and still unnumbered.

The Carolina byways are among the most inviting in all this lovely land and rewarding to wander in any season.

But go slow enough.

Painted Trillium, Alleghany County

Virginia

MOUNT AIRY

DANBURY

Paralleling
the Blue Ridge
Parkway

Mountain
roads to
Glendale
Springs

Mount Airy
to Blue
Ridge
Parkway

Back
roads
to Mount
Airy

Road through
Stone Mt.
Park

GLENDALE SPRINGS

New River
back road

Roads from
Banner Elk
to Valle Crucis

BOONE

VALLE
CRUCIS

Wilkesboro
to Glendale
Springs

WILKESBORO

BANNER
ELK

BLOWING
ROCK

LINVILLE

Back roads to
Blowing Rock
and Linville

North Carolina back roads

SPRUCE
PINE

Back roads to
Zebulon Vances
birthplace

Tennessee

DILLINGHAM

Blue Ridge Parkway

40

HICKORY

Central North Carolina

40

ASHEVILLE

Western

BRYSON
CITY

CHEROKEE

Along the
Tuckasegee
to the
Cullasaja

HENDERSONVILLE

RUTHERFORDTON

Back road to
Connemara

FLAT
ROCK

Flat Rock
to Rutherfordton

CASHIERS

Road
through
Pisgan
Forest

CEDAR
MT.

HIGHLANDS

QUEBEC

South Carolina

Georgia

Highlands
to Cashiers

Old Mill of Guilford, Guilford County

Western North Carolina

With 43 summits more than 6,000 feet high, western North Carolina's mountains are a dramatic and impressive sight. Between the mountain towns and communities is a plenitude of back roads. Plain dirt ones are my favorites. They look as if they really belong in the landscape, especially those that simply follow the contour of the land without deep cuts on either side. Next I prefer gravel roads and, last, paved roads that are not too wide and do not have stripes painted down the middle. Stripes, of course, are a safety measure and with our propensity to go ever faster from place to place, they are a good thing. I'm thankful, however, for the few less-traveled, unmarked dirt roads that remain. I can travel them slowly enough to appreciate the wildflowers, the sunlight glinting through the trees, and the fresh, bright green of new spring leaves.

12

Hanging Rock, Stokes County

I stop at Old Mill of Guilford on my way to Hanging Rock State Park. Back roads do not really begin this close to Greensboro, although the historic old waterpowered gristmill certainly belongs on one. In keeping with its 200-year-old tradition, the genial owner, Mr. Charles Parnell, offers for sale water-ground and stone-ground flour, cornmeal, whole wheat, rye, oats, bran, wheat germ, and grits (among other items), all without preservatives.

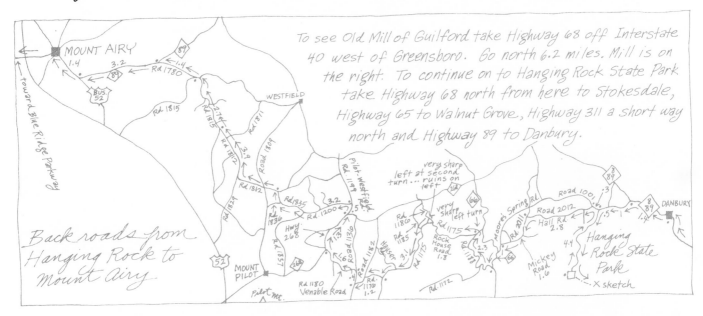

To see Old Mill of Guilford take Highway 68 off Interstate 40 west of Greensboro. Go north 6.2 miles. Mill is on the right. To continue on to Hanging Rock State Park take Highway 68 north from here to Stokesdale, Highway 65 to Walnut Grove, Highway 311 a short way north and Highway 89 to Danbury.

Back roads from Hanging Rock to Mount Airy.

At Hanging Rock State Park in the Sauratown Mountains I hike the trail to see the hanging rock. It is only seven-tenths of a mile to the summit but a steep climb at times. Pinxter and dogwood bloom along the way. Where Hanging Rock juts upward the trail is outlined by red marks on rocks and trees. At trail's end I am finally atop the 200-foot outcropping of quartzite. A cold, fierce wind blows at the summit and I grip my drawing board tightly as I draw rock, trees, and the Dan River valley.

There are over a dozen places to hike to see waterfalls and panoramic views at Hanging Rock State Park.

Listening to good bluegrass music from Mount Airy on my car radio and not paying strict attention to my county map, I make a wrong turn and come across the ruins of an old church (picture on page 8). Wild vines reach upward, rock upon rock, and flutter in the breeze at the top of the wall where they can climb no higher.

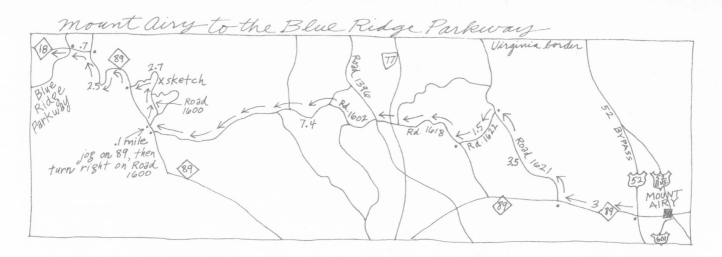

Mount Airy to the Blue Ridge Parkway

    I drive through rolling green hills of corn crops, pastureland, and forests and sketch in a deep valley cut by rushing mountain waters.

    Driving on, I connect with the Blue Ridge Parkway, one of America's great scenic highways, following mountain crests sometimes over 5,000 feet high.

    I look for back roads paralleling this famous highway, returning from time to time to travel the well-tended parklike roadway.

Painted trillium is abundant in the forest (picture, pg. 9). This unique acid-loving plant can be identified by the deep crimson blaze at the base of its wavy white petals. Its pristine beauty constrasts with the debris encountered sometimes on back roads (map, pg. 16). I go on, lifting my eyes to the trees and mountains to make myself joyful again.

Mountain Farm, Surry County

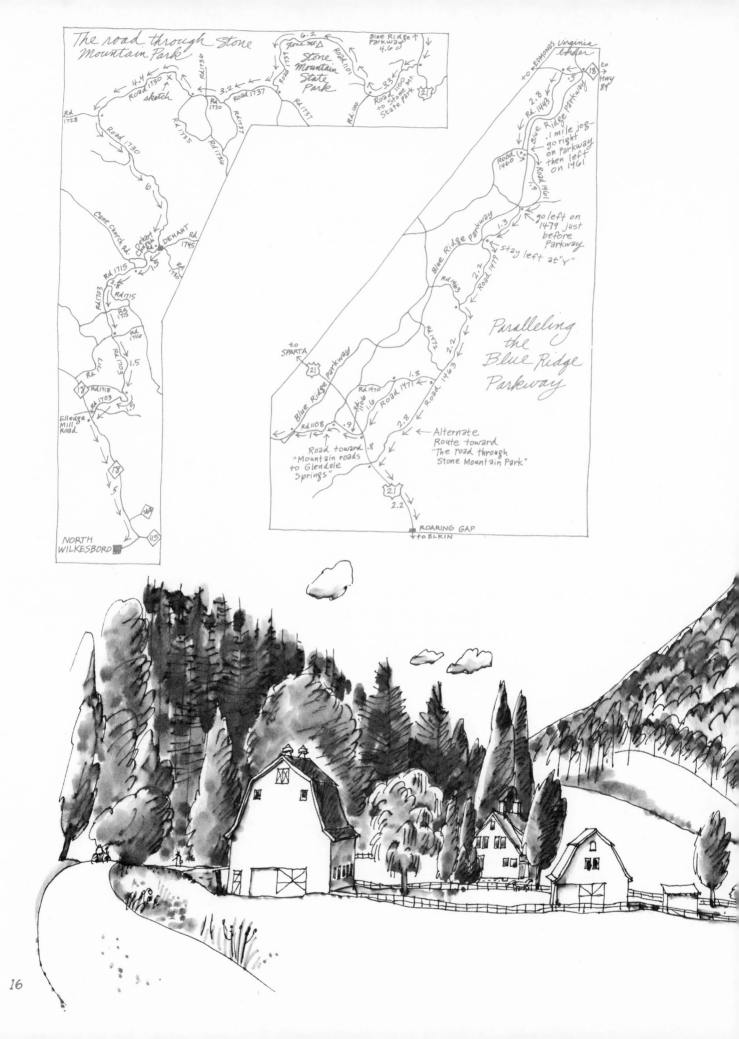

The road through Stone Mountain Park

Road 1730 sketch

4.4

Road 1730

3.2

Rd 1735

Rd 1736

Road 1737

Rd 1737

6

Rd 1728

Rd 1730

6.2

Stone Mt △

Rd 1739

Road 1101

Stone Mountain State Park

Blue Ridge Parkway 4.6

33

Road 1100 to Stone Mt. State park

Rd 1100

21

Rd 1737

Cane Church Rd.

Dehart Church Rd.

DEHART

Rd 1745

Rd 1730

1.3

Rd 1715

2.6

Rd 1703

Rd 1715

Rd. 1715

Rd 1710

1.5

Rd 717

Rd 1703

8 Rd 1718

Rd 1703

.9

Elledge Mill Road

8

5

68

115

NORTH WILKESBORO

to EDMONDS

.5

18

to Hwy 89

2.8 Rd. 1443

Blue Ridge parkway

.1 mile jog - go right on Parkway then left on 1461

Road 1460

Road 1461

.7

1.3

go left on 1479 just before Parkway

stay left at "Y"

Blue Ridge parkway

Road 1479

2.2

Rd 1463

Rd 1472

2.2

to SPARTA

21

Blue Ridge parkway

Rd 1470

Rd 1016

1.6

Road 1471

1.3

Road 1463

2.8

Paralleling the Blue Ridge Parkway

Rd 1108

.9

Road toward "Mountain roads to Glendale Springs"

.8

Alternate Route toward "The road through Stone Mountain Park"

21

2.2

ROARING GAP

to ELKIN

Virginia border

16

The road through Stone Mountain State Park

The road follows Stone Creek, where I see many men and women fishing for trout. The only traffic past the place where I stop to sketch is a very slow-moving tractor whose driver waves a welcome. He plows the field beyond at the same slow rate as I draw.

Wilkes County Landscape

Mountain roads to Glendale Springs

I draw a deserted farmhouse nestled in a deep green valley. Cows graze nearby and a mountain stream flows past the decaying old building.

On Road 1193 there is a hairpin turn to the left. Although it is picturesque, I do not recommend this road for low-slung cars or for travel in wet weather. An alternate back road route goes to Whitehead, crosses Highway 113 and follows the rushing New River upstream.

Back Road Mountain Scene,
Alleghany County

Along the way I enjoy broad vistas of mountain country, dairy land, the patterned landscape of Christmas tree farms, dogwood and apple trees in bloom, and occasional fishermen intently angling for trout.

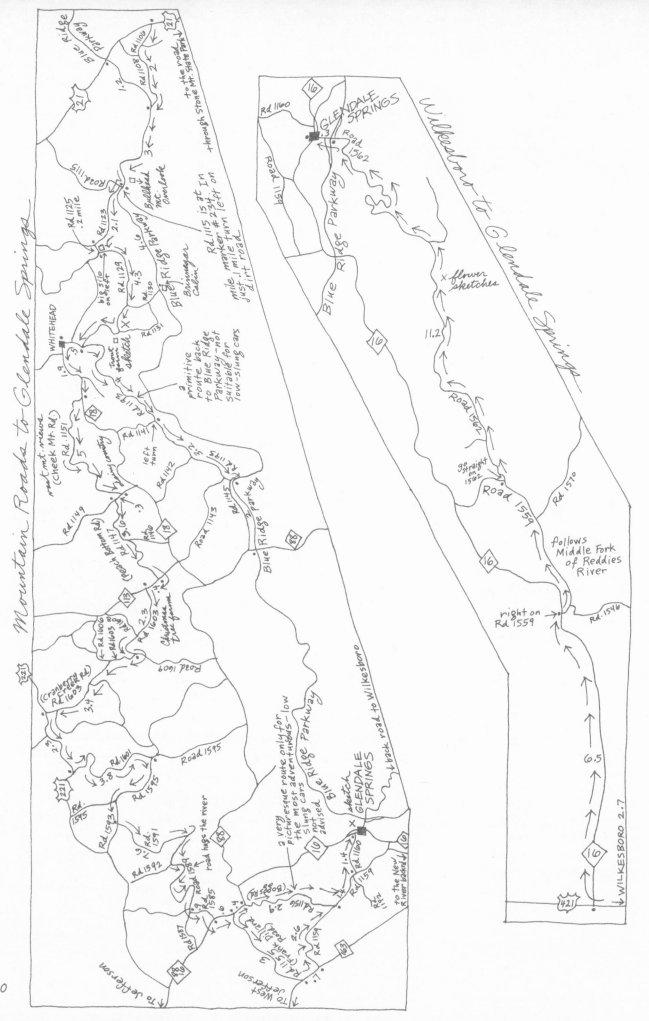

Mountain Roads to Glendale Springs

Wilkesboro to Glendale Springs

GLENDALE SPRINGS

WHITEHEAD

WILKESBORO 2.7

follows Middle Fork of Reddies River

right on Rd 1559

go straight on 1562

x flower sketches

Blue Ridge Parkway

Blue Ridge Ridge

primitive route back to Blue Ridge Parkway—not suitable for low-slung cars

a very picturesque route only for the most adventurous—low slung cars not advised

road hugs the river

Rd.1115 is at In mile marker #234 turn left on just .1 mile turn left on dirt road

to the road— through Stone Mt. State Park

20

The road follows a tumbling stream, and I cross it back and forth over one-way bridges as I proceed. Then it narrows between canyon walls, emerging into an occasional meadow and deep forests. Wild flowers are in evidence and I sketch birdfoot violets and mountain iris.

Birdfoot Violets

In Glendale Springs I stop at the Holy Trinity Church where artist Ben Long has painted an intriguing fresco of the Last Supper. My drawing detail shows a portion of it with Ben Long himself posing on the right as "doubting Thomas." The stool in the picture represents an invitation for you, the viewer, to join the supper.

As I draw I press a button to hear the recorded voice of Father Faulton Hodge describe the fresco and its history. I am deeply moved by the story and listen to it threes times during my stay. You can journey to St. Mary's Church, close by in West Jefferson, to see other frescoes by Ben Long.

Mountain Iris

Holy Trinity Church of the Fresco, Glendale Springs, Ashe County

Glendale Springs and the New River back road

On back roads I meander along with the river,
stopping to draw a bridge and a farm scene. In the
picture you can see the farmer with pail in hand
pondering what I am doing. His lady is mowing, the
dog is barking at the stranger across the river, and
in between barks I hear the chickens clucking.

   The bridges I have been crossing today tilt down
on the upstream side (I didn't put the awkward-
looking tilt in my picture, however) and later I ask
the lady why. She tells me that it helps logs and debris
to flow more easily over the bridges at high water.

   I ask if they would be dangerous to cross during
a frost. She recollects one morning when for some
reason the railing board was off one of the
bridges and a local man going to work
in his pickup slid off and sank
into the icy cold New River.

Glendale Springs and the New River back road

South Fork of the New River, Watauga County

Great banks of rhododendron drape the roadside to Blowing Rock. From there Globe Road descends steeply through dense forest freshly green with new spring growth.

The road levels off into a narrow valley where corn grows and tree nurseries flourish. There are waterfalls along the road where I begin again to ascend toward Linville and I stop to draw a particularly striking one past Gragg.

Cascading Falls, Avery County

This is a hilly trip with views of mountains and farms, forests and meadows. The road hugs the Watauga River for a time. I see a stone house nearby with at least ten millstones incorporated into its facade in an interesting way.

I draw the rippling Watauga and the scene along its banks. Girls on horseback ride by, ducks swim back and forth, and cows graze — a serene aspect of the rural mountain life of North Carolina.

In Valle Crucis the delightful 1883 Mast General Store still resists change and modernization.

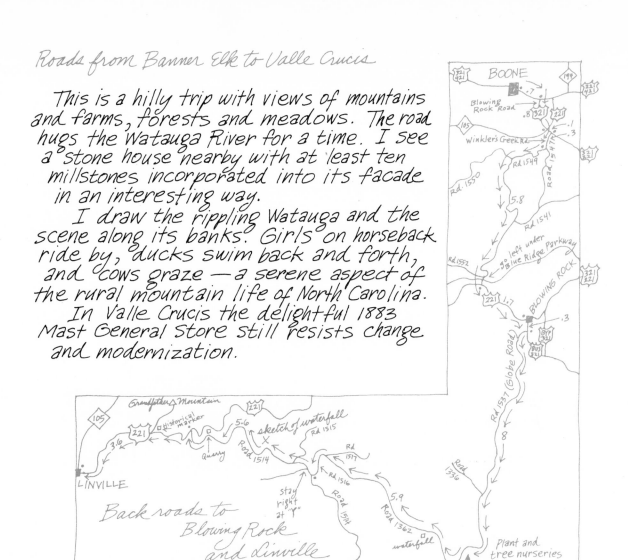

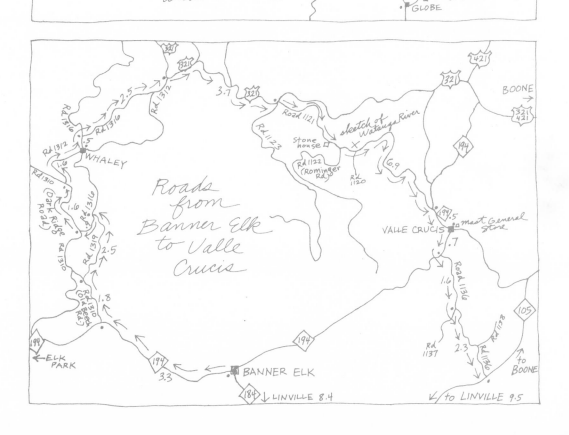

Farms along the Watauga River, Watauga County

Paint Fork Church,
Buncombe County

Back roads to Zebulon Vance's birthplace

DEMOCRAT
197

197
.2 BARNARDSVILLE

3.7

Pinnacle △ mt.
Rd 2165   Rd 2173

Rd 2173

DILLINGHAM

Road 1003

PAINT FORK

Rd 2167
(Haw Branch Road)

sketch X
of church
and graveyard

5.3

View of valley and Pinnacle Mountain

6.5

Rd 63A

Rd 1003

1.7   Rd 2115

Forest Rd 63
(dirt road)

.7   □ Vance birthplace   Rd 2114

Craggy Gardens Picnic Grounds

Rd 2109
Ox Creek Rd.

4.5   Rd 2109

back road journey begins at entrance to Craggy Gardens Picnic Grounds

2.5   □

Visitor Center Craggy Gardens

Rd 2110

dirt road

to ASHEVILLE ↓   Blue Ridge Parkway   Blue Ridge Parkway

Back roads to Zebulon Vance's birthplace

An unmarked dirt road descends from the Blue Ridge Parkway near Craggy Gardens through green forest landscape. Small streams of water tumble alongside the road on the way to the valley towns of Dillingham and Barnardsville.

Church bells are ringing for Sunday service at the little church in Paint Fork, a ritual in every village and town in these picturesque mountains. I stop to draw the tranquil scene. The church graveyard overlooks the homes, fields, and church where its occupants once lived, worked, and worshipped.

At Zebulon Vance's birthplace I discover an excellent grouping of historic log structures. David Vance homesteaded this land in 1795. He was a revolutionary soldier, lawyer, surveyor, teacher, and grandfather of North Carolina's famous Civil War governor, Zebulon B. Vance, who was born here on May 13, 1830.

31

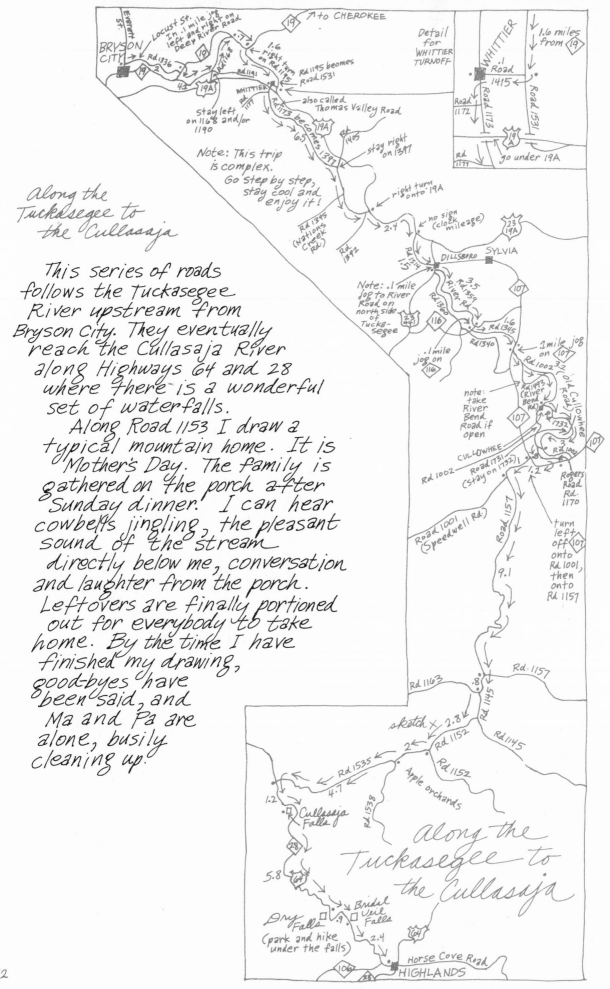

Along the
Tuckasegee to
the Cullasaja

This series of roads
follows the Tuckasegee
River upstream from
Bryson City. They eventually
reach the Cullasaja River
along Highways 64 and 28
where there is a wonderful
set of waterfalls.

Along Road 1153 I draw a
typical mountain home. It is
Mother's Day. The family is
gathered on the porch after
Sunday dinner. I can hear
cowbells jingling, the pleasant
sound of the stream
directly below me, conversation
and laughter from the porch.
Leftovers are finally portioned
out for everybody to take
home. By the time I have
finished my drawing,
good-byes have
been said, and
Ma and Pa are
alone, busily
cleaning up.

Mountain Home, Jackson County

Whiteside Mountain, Jackson County

Highlands to Cashiers

I leave the handsome village of Highlands on Horse Cove Road, a continuation of Main Street. Along this road are views of 4,930-foot Whiteside Mountain, its sheer cliffs the highest in the eastern United States.

The Chattooga River, featured in the movie "Deliverance," has its source here and I cross the young stream along the way.

After making a drawing of the tremendous rock face of Whiteside, I continue on to the mountain town of Cashiers near Lake Toxaway.

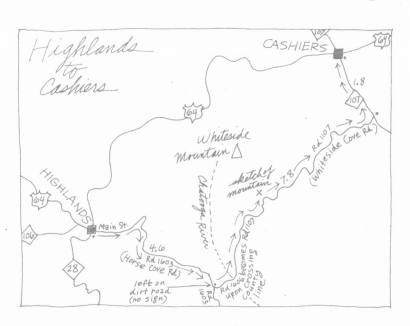

Back road through Pisgah National Wildlife Area

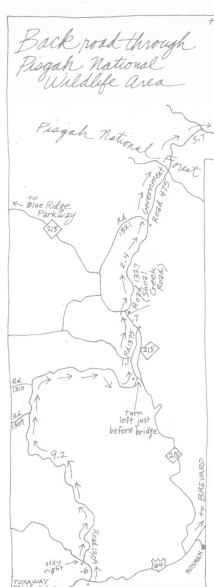

Back road through Pisgah National Wildlife Area

to Blue Ridge Parkway

Cradle of Forestry in America (276)

Sliding Rock

Looking Glass Falls

2.2

.4

to BREVARD 276

Pisgah National Forest

5.7

Pisgah Forest National Fish Hatchery

1.4

3.9 to Ranger Station

to Blue Ridge Parkway 215

Rd 1321

Government Road 475

2.4

Road 1327 (Shoal Creek Road)

.7

Rd 1375

215

Rd 1310

Rd 1309

9.2

turn left just before bridge

215

Road 1309

stay right .6

64

ROSMAN

to BREVARD

TOXAWAY FALLS 4.6

Back road through Pisgah National Wildlife Area

The road traverses a pretty valley as it follows the French Broad River, then connects with Pisgah forest roads. I stop to watch hungry rainbow trout being fed at Pisgah Forest National Fish Hatchery. Looking Glass Falls and Sliding Rock are other attractions along the way to the Cradle of Forestry Visitor Center. The center honors the establishment of the first school of forestry in the United States.

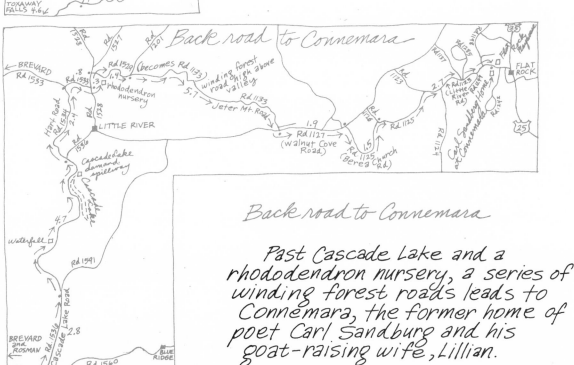

Back road to Connemara

Rd 1528 Rd 1527 Rd 1201

Rd 1529 (becomes Rd 1133)

BREVARD Rd 1533

.8 1.4

Rd 1533 .3 rhododendron nursery

Hart Road Rd 1534 2.4

Rd 1528

Rd 1536

LITTLE RIVER

Cascade Lake dam and spillway

Cascade Lake

4.7

Waterfall

Rd 1591

winding forest road high above valley

5.7

Rd 1133 Jeter Mt. Road

1.9

Rd 1127 (Walnut Cove Road)

1.5 Rd 1125 (Berea Church Rd.)

Rd 1125

Rd 1124

Rd 1123

2.7

Rd 1246 Rd 1178

Rd 1197

Rd 1125 Little River Ralph Rd

FLAT ROCK

Carl Sandburg Home at Connemara

Rd 1244

25

BREVARD and ROSMAN

Rd 1536 Cascade Lake Road 2.8

276 Rd 1560 BLUE RIDGE

CEDAR MOUNTAIN

215

Back road to Connemara

Past Cascade Lake and a rhododendron nursery, a series of winding forest roads leads to Connemara, the former home of poet Carl Sandburg and his goat-raising wife, Lillian.

I park and walk the uphill path to the Sandburg house. The tour goes from room to room, and with the family furniture all still in place, Sandburg's presence is truly felt. I expect Carl to peer around a doorway at any moment and gruffly ask what we are doing in his house!
  There are short trails to hike here, paths that Carl would surely walk were he still here.

Flat Rock to Rutherfordton

note: Road 1850, though quite scenic, has a muddy spot. Take Road 1852 and Road 9832 if it looks impassable.

9
1.7
jog right on 9, then left on 1161
Rd 1161
Rd 1161
Rd 1310
Road 1311
Rd 1315
(Lake Adger Road) Rd 1138
sketch of mailbox
7.5
Rd 1156
6.9
Lake Adger
Rd 1155
Rd 1151
Rd 1138 (no sign)
Rd 1311
108
to RUTHERFORDTON 9.9
9
108
MILL SPRING

176
EAST FLAT ROCK
26
FLAT ROCK
Connemara Sandburg Home
25 3.4
Highway 25 go under Rd 1207
25
TUXEDO
Rd 1852 (alternate route)
Rd 1852
Rd 1850 (S. Lake Summit Rd.)
Pace Mt. Road
.5
Hotherly Heights Rd.
Rd 1806
4.9
muddy spot
SALUDA
176
2.1
Rd 1142 on 1142
Rd 1141
(Alternate route) Rd 1151
Holberts Cove Road 10.2 Rd 1142
26
108
VALHALLA
2.3
Pearson Falls Rd.
Rd 1102
Tunnel
Rd 1100
1.6
2
1.4
Rd 1840 Rd 1841 Rd 1181
Pearson's Falls Nature Preserve
176
TRYON

Flat Rock to Rutherfordton

From Carl Sandburg's home I travel interesting back roads on my way east. I come to a bad spot along one very scenic road.
  Recent rains have created a mud hole across the entire width of the road. I run at it in my little car and slither to the other side, mud-spattered but safely across. I offer an alternative to this route on my map.
  I pass Pearson's Falls Nature Preserve, drive through a short one-way tunnel, follow a twisting mountain road and cross Lake Adger. Near the community of Sunny View, southeast of Lake Lure, I sketch a humorous homemade mailbox stand.

U.S. MAIL

Polk County

Connemara, Henderson County

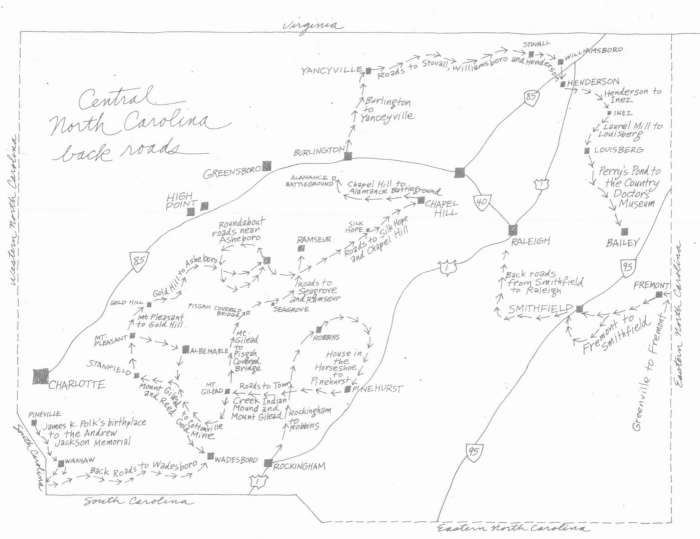

Central
North Carolina
back roads

Virginia

YANCYVILLE → Roads to Stovall, Williamsboro and Henderson → STOVALL → WILLIAMSBORO

↑ Burlington to Yanceyville

HENDERSON
→ Henderson to Inez
■ INEZ
↓ Laurel Mill to Louisberg
■ LOUISBERG
Perry's Pond to the Country Doctor's Museum

BURLINGTON

GREENSBORO

ALAMANCE BATTLEGROUND
Chapel Hill to Alamance Battleground

CHAPEL HILL

HIGH POINT

Roundabout roads near Asheboro

RAMSEUR

SILK HOPE
Roads to Silk Hope and Chapel Hill

RALEIGH

BAILEY

Gold Hill to Asheboro

Roads to Seagrove and Ramseur

Back roads from Smithfield to Raleigh

FREMONT

GOLD HILL

PISGAH COVERED BRIDGE

SEAGROVE

SMITHFIELD

Mt Pleasant to Gold Hill

Fremont to Smithfield

MT. PLEASANT

ALBEMARLE

Mt. Gilead to Pisgah Covered Bridge

ROBBINS

House in the Horseshoe to Pinehurst

STANFIELD

CHARLOTTE

Mount Gilead and Reed Gold Mine

MT. GILEAD

Roads to Town

PINEHURST

PINEVILLE
James K. Polk's birthplace to the Andrew Jackson Memorial

Mt. Gilead to Cottonville

Creek Indian Mound and Mount Gilead

Rockingham to Robbins

WAXHAW

Back Roads to Wadesboro

WADESBORO

ROCKINGHAM

Greenville to Fremont

South Carolina

Eastern North Carolina

Western North Carolina

Cardinal

Central North Carolina

The midlands encompass the
Piedmont section of North Carolina,
an area of gently rolling hills of
trees and green grass underlaid
with reddish earth. Through
agricultural lands and lush forests
the back roads weave.

To me, the drive to wherever I am
bound is equal in interest to the place
itself. What can I see along the way that
is new, different, charming, or beautiful?
That is the challenge. I need only a good county
map as a guide and a leisurely journey that
allows me time enough to enjoy whatever I find
interesting along the way. I feel privileged to be
able to travel from place to place in comfort
and without restrictions.

There are countless roads going in all
directions. I hope you will truly enjoy the
ones I have chosen.

Near Pineville I visit the memorial to James K. Polk, the eleventh president of the United States. He was born here in 1795 and spent his childhood on the 250-acre farm worked by his parents. Log buildings and furnishings of the early 1800s are part of the memorial.

I travel on to Waxhaw where, in an outdoor amphitheater, the Revolutionary War drama "Listen and Remember" is performed during the summer.

At Andrew Jackson State Park I sketch an early 19th-century schoolhouse built by a Mr. Henry Boswell. He later lost his life in the War Between the States, but his sturdy schoolhouse still stands beneath the trees. Nearby is a statue of Andrew Jackson as a youth by sculptor Anna Huntington.

At the museum in the park I enjoy reading some of Andrew Jackson's letters. In one, written to James H. Witherspoon, Esq., on August 11, 1824, Jackson locates his birthplace "at the plantation whereon James Crawford lived about one mile from the Carolina road x-ing of the Waxhaw Creek."

The Old Schoolhouse, Andrew Jackson State Park

Whether Jackson was born in North or South Carolina is still in question, it seems. According to my county map detail, the state park appears to be in North Carolina, whereas the road into the park is in South Carolina.

I stop to see the well-preserved collection at the Mexico Museum, which includes a restored 1938 Chevrolet — a gift from Lázaro Cárdenas, president of Mexico from 1934 to 1940.

James K. Polk's birthplace to the Andrew Jackson Memorial

to Interstate 77
521 to CHARLOTTE
77 PINEVILLE 51
34
James K. Polk Birthplace
Lancaster Highway
2.9
521
Rd 3626
Rd 3632
Rd 3635
4.3
Marvin Rd.
Rd 1313 Rd 1316
Rd 1312 MARVIN
Rd 1315½ Rd 1315
New Town Road
Rd 1307 Rd 1304
Rd 1307
16
7.4
Rd 1304
South Carolina
leave on North Main
Rd 1301
WAXHAW
75 Main St. 75
1.6 .3
listen and Remember Theatre
2.6 Rd 1107 Rd 1111
Rd 1108
1.2 round church Rd 1113
Rd 1112
Rd 1117 (Providence Road)
Rd 1107 (Rehobeth Ch.)
.9
Davis Rd.
Rd 1117
JACKSON
Xsketch Rd 1105
.3
Mexico Museum
200
Rd 1128
Andrew Jackson Memorial
2.5 2.5
4.5
Rd 1104
Rd 1106
200
note: you can visit Mex. Museum from here or later from Waxhaw
Rd 1102
Rd 1104 (Waxhaw Church Rd.)
Rd 1100 (Tirzah Church Rd.)
1.8 .4
200
South Carolina

Back roads to Wadesboro

I travel back roads to Trinity community, where I draw a typical farmhouse and barn of the area.

Farm Landscape, Union County

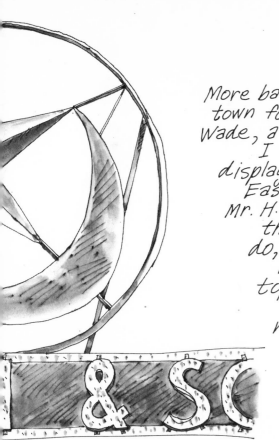

More back roads bring me to Wadesboro, an attractive town founded in 1783 and named for Captain Thomas Wade, a local Revolutionary War patriot.
I am intrigued by the sheet metal patterns displayed at Marsh & Sons Sheet Metal Works at East Washington and East Morgan streets.
Mr. H. F. Marsh tells me how he came to make the skillful sculptural designs. "The more you do, the further you want to go," he says.
His tin woodsman has been waving from the top of his roof for many years. It is his trademark. The first tin woodsman he made, however, had been stolen by Halloween pranksters, hoisted on a pole, accidentally dropped, and ruined.

Sheet Metal Sign, Wadesboro, Anson County

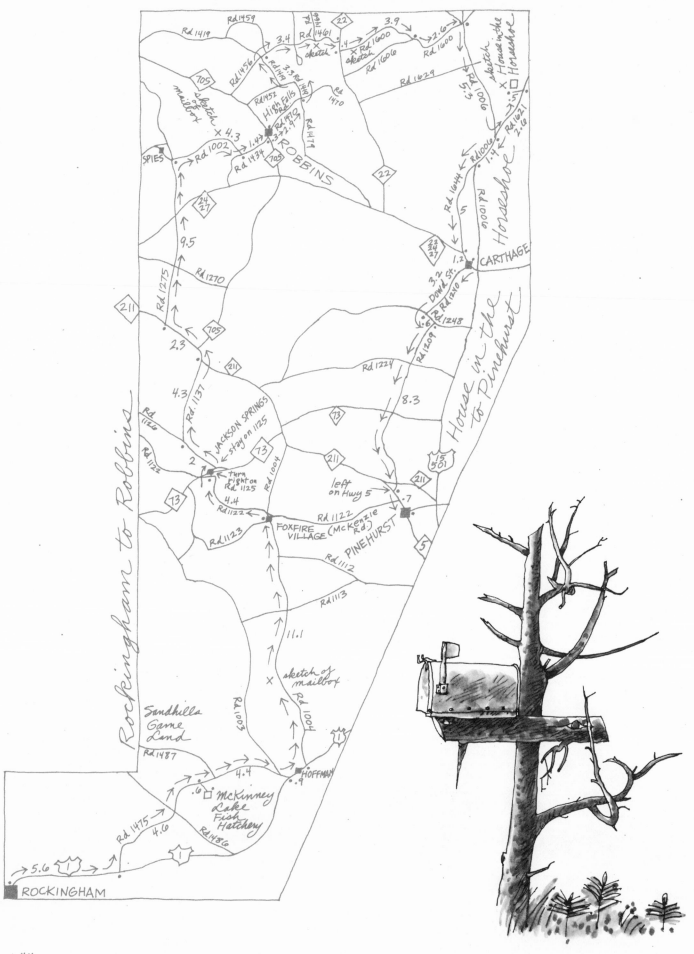

Rockingham to Robbins

Going through Sandhills Game Land I
stop at McKinney Lake National Fish
Hatchery. Bluegills, largemouth bass,
striped bass, redear bream, catfish,
and perch are raised until they are
big enough to be trucked to the
warmwater ponds and streams of
North Carolina. There is also a
well-stocked yellow-bellied
turtle pen here.
     I approach Hoffman village between
lines of magnolia and dogwood trees. I see
a black squirrel, pass a dead possum (they
lumber on to roads at night, not heeding traffic),
and stop to draw a series of creative mailbox stands.

I cross a succession of lovely
streams and rivers along
these hilly, green
country roads.

Deep River wends its way in a horseshoe shape around the Alston House and land (thus the name House in the Horseshoe). It was here that a skirmish occurred between a band of patriots under Colonel Phillip Alston and the Tories under David Fanning on July 29, 1781. Mrs. Alston, I am told, hid her children in the big fireplace and then put the table upright against it so they would be protected during the fighting. I sketch the front door with the original bullet holes scattered around it.

At Carthage (map, page 44), in the circle, a stone shaft honors Roger McConnell, a local citizen who died serving in the French army in 1917.

Entrance to House in the Horseshoe, Moore County

Town Creek Indian Mound, Montgomery County

In Pinehurst, I find stately pines, flowering dogwood, handsome houses, and exquisitely trimmed gardens. I read that there are 24 golf courses within a 20-mile radius. Frederick Law Olmsted, designer of Central Park in New York City and Asheville's Biltmore Gardens, laid out these New England-style parks and roadways. This is also the home of the World Golf Hall of Fame.

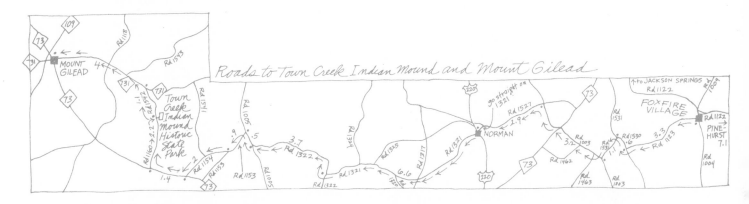

Roads to Town Creek Indian Mound and Mount Gilead

Roads to Town Creek Indian Mound and Mount Gilead

Driving through forests and past grainfields and neatly pruned peach orchards, I arrive at Town Creek Indian Mound. Indians migrated here in about A.D. 1500 and built a ceremonial center. I walk across a broad grass clearing to see the Indian temple buildings whose reconstruction was based on intensive archaeological research. The Visitor Center also shows orientation slides.

My back road journey then continues to the pleasant town of Mount Gilead.

Mount Gilead to Cottonville, and the Reed Gold Mine

The local minister tells me that Cottonville was quite a busy crossroads in Revolutionary times. Today it is a quiet place.

I continue traveling over the pretty, green rolling country to Stanfield and Locust communities and to the Reed Gold Mine. I tour the mine and sketch Little Meadow Creek where gold was discovered in 1799, the first authenticated gold find in the United States. Story has it that farmer John Reed's son had played hooky from church one Sunday and found a yellow rock in the creek. It subsequently served as a doorstop in the Reed home and is purported to have weighed 17 pounds. In 1802 a jeweler in Fayetteville recognized the rock as gold, melted it down and formed the metal into a bar. He paid Reed $3.50 for it—one-tenth of one percent of its value. However, years later Reed made up for his folly by becoming rich.

There is a Visitor Center with the museum. Guests also have the opportunity to actually pan for gold, the original method used by Reed and his partners when the Reed Gold Mine was established.

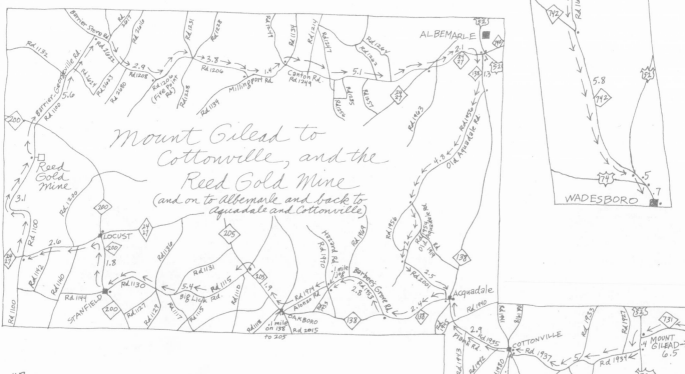

Mount Gilead to Cottonville, and the Reed Gold Mine
(and on to Albemarle and back to Aquadale and Cottonville)

Little Meadow Creek, Cabarrus County

Mount Gilead to Pisgah Covered Bridge

I travel forest roads and good dirt roads to Pisgah Covered Bridge. Initials carved into the old alder tree in front of the bridge have begun to disappear. As the tree has grown, the carvings have been incorporated into its overall bark pattern. Not so the graffiti on the dead wood of the old bridge. It will stay until erosion erases it or the bridge is restored.

This is a quiet place with only the sound of a gurgling creek to break the silence. The bridge is no longer used, having been replaced by an uninteresting looking but more practical one beside it. Once Randolph County had more covered bridges than any other county in North Carolina. Only Pisgah and a few others are left to remind us of another day, another time.

50

Pisgah Covered Bridge, Randolph County

51

Mount Gilead to Pisgah Covered Bridge

ASHEBORO
10.8 ↑

Rd 1143

Rd 1112
Rd 1111
Rd 1109   Rd 1127
1.6   PISGAH

to SEAGROVE →

Rd 1109 →
no sign for turnoff →   Rd 1111
Rd 181

Rd 1107   ↑ 2.6
Rd 1108
dirt road   □X

Piagah Covered Bridge

5.2   Rd 1111
Rd 1304
Rd 1134   Rd 1305
(dirt road)   Rd 1114

.6

OPHIR   Rd 1306

historic church

Rd 1303   Rd 1134
(dirt road)

East Morris
Mt. Camp

Rd 1314

7.8

109   Rd 1134

Rd 1146   Rd 1144
Rd 1139

6.3
Rd 1134   Rd 1137

24 27

← sign for "PEE DEE"
1

Rd 1130   Rd 1134
Rd 1133
3.4   Rd 1174

Rd 1130

Edmund Deberry home 1787-1859

Rd 1128
2.2   109

73   1.3

MOUNT GILEAD

731

Roads to
Seagrove and
Ramseur

Country roads bring us to Seagrove where North Carolina potters have lived and worked since the time of the early settlers. At Seagrove Pottery Museum, where the work of the early potters is displayed, I draw two whiskey pots, one dating from 1787, the other from 1870. The squat-type pot was used for transporting liquor in wagons and carriages as it was spillproof, especially when fitted with a good corncob-and-cloth stopper, the way this one is. The museum's fine collection is housed in the former local train depot next to Seagrove Pottery.

I drive through Whynot, one mile from Seagrove. When the time came to name the post office so many people asked, "Why not name it (this)" or "Why not name it (that)?" that the townsfolk finally settled on the first two words of their question. And I agree. Why not!

Whiskey Pots,
Seagrove,
Randolph
County

In Ramseur my short tour of the hilly town goes out Main Street. Near the bottom of the hill, I turn left at Factory Road, past the historic cotton mill. I keep going to Salisbury Street and then back to town.

Roads to Seagrove and Ramseur

I see many fine old houses along Main Street in Mount Pleasant. The town is known for two historic institutions— Mount Amoena (meaning Mount Pleasant) Seminary for Women (1859-1927), and Mount Pleasant Collegiate Institute for Men (1903-33). Both can be found on the North Main Street site of North Carolina College (1853-1902).

Mount Pleasant has an old water tower—painted a soft baby blue— which I draw in my profile of the town.

I journey next to Gold Hill, where gold was discovered in 1824. By 1843 the place had become a boomtown.

Copper was mined there until 1907.

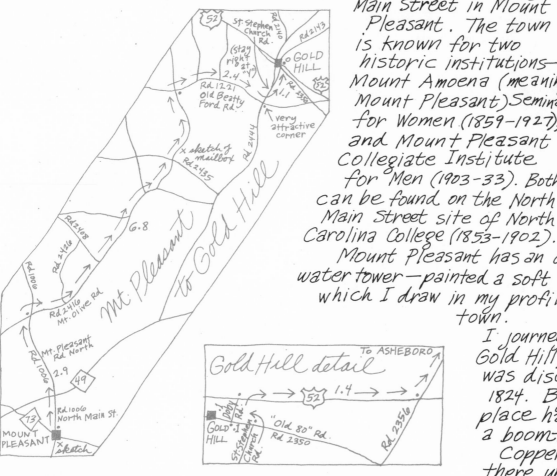

Sunken Telephone Pole Mailbox

Gold Hill to Asheboro

    I continue from Gold Hill on my farm and forest drive. Sweet meadow aromas fill the air. At Yadkin River there is a good view of the dam on the left. Fishermen line the shores.

    Cypress trees edge fields of green and, as I drive these back roads, I see neatly painted houses and well-clipped gardens alive with colorful flowers and white dogwood. In contrast, old barns and pioneer homes, their wood almost blackened with age, seem in the process of being consumed by vines and completely hidden by trees.

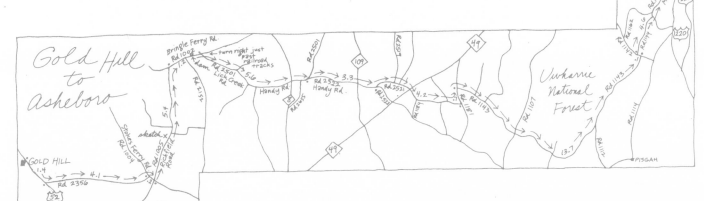

Roundabout roads near Asheboro

The scenery is rural and picturesque. I locate
Skeen's Covered Bridge to one side of Road 1406.
It is inaccessible and all but hidden by trees
and brush.
On another quiet back road I draw a typical
barn of this region. It is a calm place. No one
passes by during my two-hour stay.

Tumbling Down Farmhouse, Rowan County

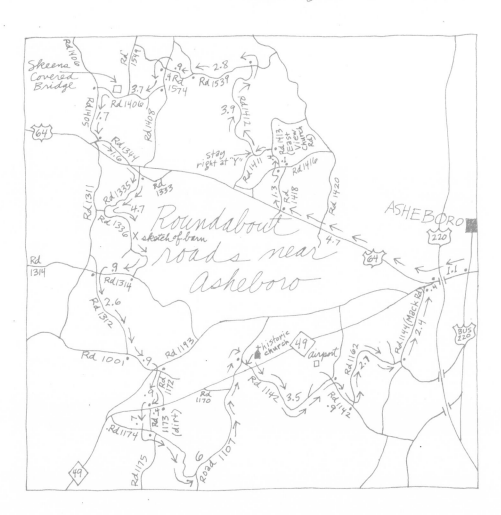

Roundabout roads near Asheboro

Barn west of Asheboro, Randolph County

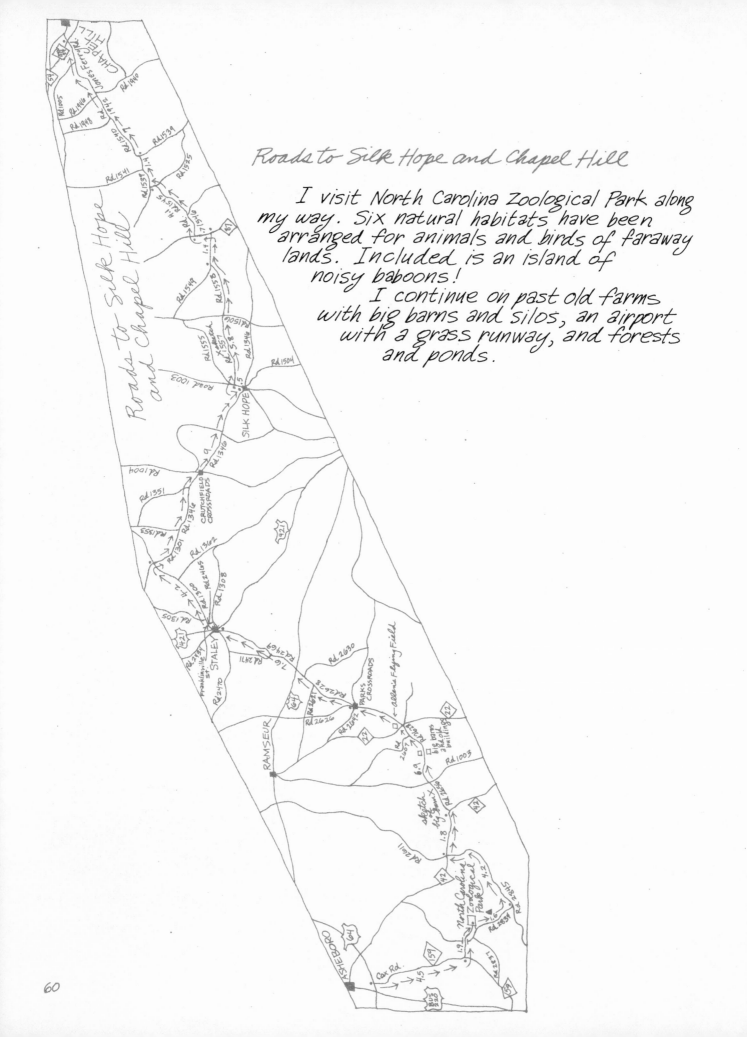

Roads to Silk Hope and Chapel Hill

I visit North Carolina Zoological Park along my way. Six natural habitats have been arranged for animals and birds of faraway lands. Included is an island of noisy baboons!

I continue on past old farms with big barns and silos, an airport with a grass runway, and forests and ponds.

Big Barn, Randolph County

Landscape near Silk Hope, Chatham County

Past Silk Hope I draw a farm scene. I show it to the owners of the farm and they tell me that the old building on the left was "Grandaddy's store" many years ago. A second story was added later to make it suitable for curing tobacco.

Old Greenwood Road is a fairly fast secondary road. Near Snow Camp I draw a barn and a tree. Trees and barns are everywhere on back roads. I have many more to draw before my journey ends. Farther along I find a marvelous primitively designed "Worms" sign to draw.

Alamance Battleground commemorates a time previous to the Revolutionary War when there was dissatisfaction among the colonists because of excessive taxation, dishonest officials, and illegal fees. The disgruntled colonists formed a large association and called themselves the "Regulators." They caused so much trouble for the royal government that Governor Tryon sent the militia to put them down. The deciding battle took place on this spot, where the Regulators were defeated. There is a tall granite monument here, dated 1880, also a historic cabin called the Allen House, and a Visitor Center.

Chapel Hill to Alamance Battleground

Barn near Snow Camp, Alamance County

Burlington to Yancyville

I stop to sketch a log tobacco barn. Vines cover one side of it, tightly clinging to the still sturdy old structure. And while I draw there are tuneful sounds from a variety of songbirds.

Around Milesville are many log buildings, a veritable bonanza of early North Carolina rural architecture. Some have been conquered by vines and storms and have tumbled into a heap.

In the town square at Yancyville I sketch the statue of a Confederate soldier. The inscription reads, "To the sons of Caswell County who served in the war of 1861—1865 in answer to the call of their country. In whatever event that may face our national existence may God give us the will to do what is right, that, like our forefathers, we may impress our times with the sincerity and steadfastness of our lives."

Tobacco Barn, Caswell County

Roads to Stovall, Williamsboro and Henderson (Map #1)

Rd. 1512

TRIPLE SPRINGS

49

4.4

Rd 1512

170

.3

501

4.5

WOODSDALE

Rd 1326

Rd 1332

Rd 1333

.2

3.1

CEFO

Rd 1337

Rd 1336

Rd 1340

Rd 1334

1.3

3.7

57

57

3.4

Solomon Rd 1561

119

2.1

Osmond Rd 1562

119

4.8

Rd 1564

Stephentown Rd.

4.3

Rd 1505
Longs Mill Rd.
X sketch of course

Rd 1577

62

1.5

Slade Rd. X sketch
Rd 1521

2.2

Rd 1579 Country Home Rd.
2.8

Firetower (Firetower Rd.)

Rd 1589

YANCYVILLE
(I left town from Main St.
I went on North St (Rd 1542))

North St.

62

86

46

Rd. 1156

Roads to Stovall, Williamsboro and Henderson (Map #2)

39

WILLIAMSBORO

39

7.8

85

858

HENDERSON
BUS
158

85

Rd 1529

sketch of
church
X

3.1

Rd 1335

.2

Rd 1303

Rd 1510

4.4

Rd 1430

Rd 1515

STOVALL

15

Rd.
1430

15

Rd 1431

.5

Rd 1430

Rd 1415

2.6

Rd 1300

Rd 1410

4.9

Rd 1403

2.3

96

Rd 1332

1.6

49

Rd 1328

8.4

Rd 1509

49

TRIPLE SPRINGS

Rd 1504

Roads to Stovall, Williamsboro, and Henderson

Cows pose for a sketch along these rural roads. Big, dark eyes stare into mine. Fortunately, the cows stay curious long enough for me to draw them.

View from Hamer, Caswell County

There are well-cared-for old houses on the back streets of Stovall. I find it interesting to tour the streets of a town to see its state of preservation and its features, and I like to stop and talk with local residents. Asking directions is one way to get acquainted.

At Williamsboro I draw St. John's Church, whose congregation was formed in 1746. The first rector, Reverend Charles Cupples, had been sent here from London that year by the Society for the Propagation of the Gospel. The building itself dates from 1757, making it the oldest frame church in North Carolina.

St. John's Church, Williamsboro, Vance County

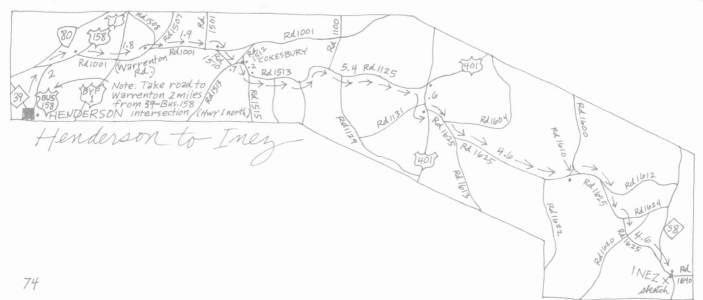

Henderson to Inez

Note: Take road to Warrenton 2 miles from 39–Bus.158 HENDERSON intersection (Hwy 1 north)

Henderson to Inez

At Inez I see a lovely plantation house sitting grandly
back of the main road. It is called Cherry Hill because
in 1858, when the place was built, the cherry orchards
around here were especially noteworthy. Today, crops
of the area are tobacco, corn, and cotton.
This historic place is still occupied by the
descendants of the original family. Out back
stand four "dependencies"— the small
square houses—that were built in
1858 to serve the main house.

They were used for storing
wood, cooking for the main
house, doing laundry and other
practical tasks.
I ask at Cherry Hill how
the house was saved from
destruction during the Civil
War. It is suggested that
perhaps the ladies somehow
successfully entertained
the Northern soldiers and
persuaded them not to
pillage their home.

Cherry Hill Plantation, Inez, Warren County

Laurel Mill, Franklin County

Inez to Laurel Mill, Louisburg, and Perry's Pond

The waters of Sandy Creek churn and froth as they pass over the dam at Laurel Mill. Bill Holmes has just gotten his first good corn of the year and is ready to grind some for visitors. He has restored the 1849 mill to working condition and it is a joy to see. The interior hums with the turning of the turbine which generates power for his home nearby. Holmes regulates the flow of water by adjusting the turbine gates and at full speed the mill can grind 400 pounds of corn in an hour.

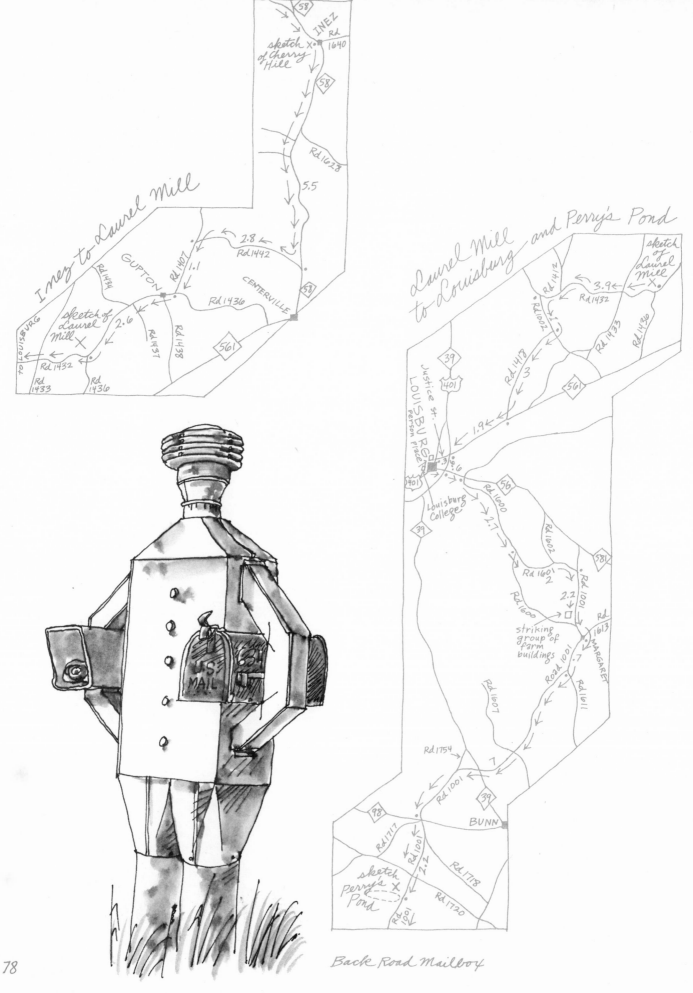

Back Road Mailbox

Beyond Laurel Mill I reach the attractive town of Louisburg, home of Louisburg College. Adjacent to the college is the restored Person Place, a focal point of historical and architectural interest for Franklin County.

The National Whistlers' Convention, held annually in Louisburg, offers seminars, and performances of classical and contemporary music, birdcalls, animal noises, and other unique sounds. I was sorry to have just missed it!

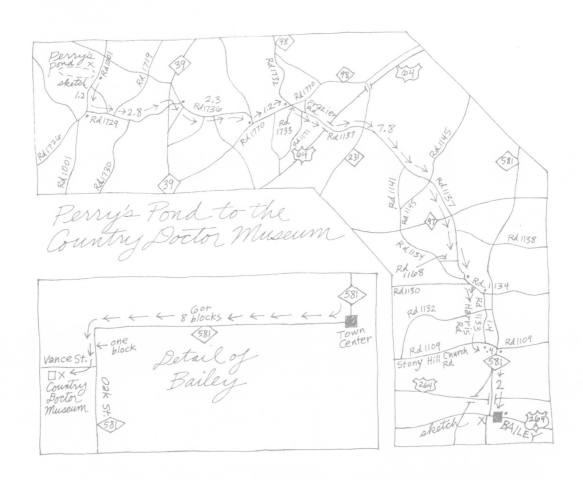

Perry's Pond to the Country Doctor Museum

The 18th-century mill at Perry's Pond is not operative; however, the millpond, stream, trees, and green grass make a picturesque setting indeed. People like to fish for bass, bream, and crappie up and down Norris Creek near the pond, and painters and photographers find inspiration in the old mill site.

Mr. Perry tells me that outdoor weddings, with the mill and falls as background, are also popular here.

Perry's Pond, Franklin County

Bone Saw,
Country Doctor
Museum

Perry's Pond to the Country Doctor Museum

I take back roads to Bailey and the Country Doctor Museum, the only one in the United States dedicated to family doctors. Their lives still inspire today's physicians. I sketch some of the interesting items from the museum collection, including a country doctor's bag and a container for leeches. The leeches were applied to a patient's skin after it had been rubbed with blood. They dropped off when they were full. An artificial leech was called a scarificator, a good name for what it was—a bloodletting device.

Doctor's Leech
Container

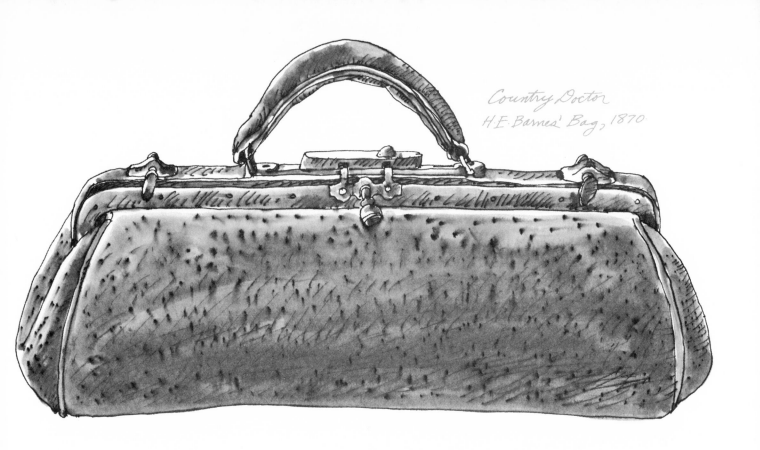

Country Doctor
H.E. Barnes' Bag, 1870.

I also draw *Matthew Moore Butler's* bone saw.
Butler was a medical doctor from 1838 to 1913 and
assisted at the amputation of General Stonewall
Jackson's left arm. I suppose it is possible that this
is the actual saw he used. The museum is filled
with fascinating items like these. A medicinal
garden out back contains plants used for healing.

The Scarificator

Near Fremont town is the restored birthplace of Charles B. Aycock (1859-1912). Carolinians are justly proud of this country-born-and-bred pioneer who went on to a career in politics and later defended certain civil liberties and campaigned for better public school education. By the end of Aycock's four-year term as governor, the state school system had been improved with many new schools and better teachers and supervisors. There is a Visitor Center here, an old schoolhouse, and the restored Aycock country home where I sketch the old kitchen hearth.

Back road routes divide along the way to Smithfield. I first take the shorter route to see the Teacherage, where Ava Gardner, the youngest of seven children, lived from age 2 to 13. Her mother was cook for the teachers at the neighboring school. In the 1920s and early 1930s Ava occasionally went to the movies in Smithfield with the teachers. Once she saw Clark Gable and Jean Harlow in "Red Dust."

In the Kitchen, Charles Aycock Birthplace near Fremont, Wayne County

Years later she herself would play opposite Gable in a remake of the film, retitled "Mogambo." An Ava Gardner museum, dedicated to the movie star, is open in the summertime to visitors.

Smithfield and Selma are historic towns with much to see. Walking-tour brochures are available from the chamber of commerce.

Bentonville Battlefield was the site of the largest battle fought in North Carolina between the North and the South. The farm home of John and Amy Harper was used as a field hospital for Union and, later, Confederate soldiers. The house is still there as are a Confederate cemetery and a section of Union trenches.

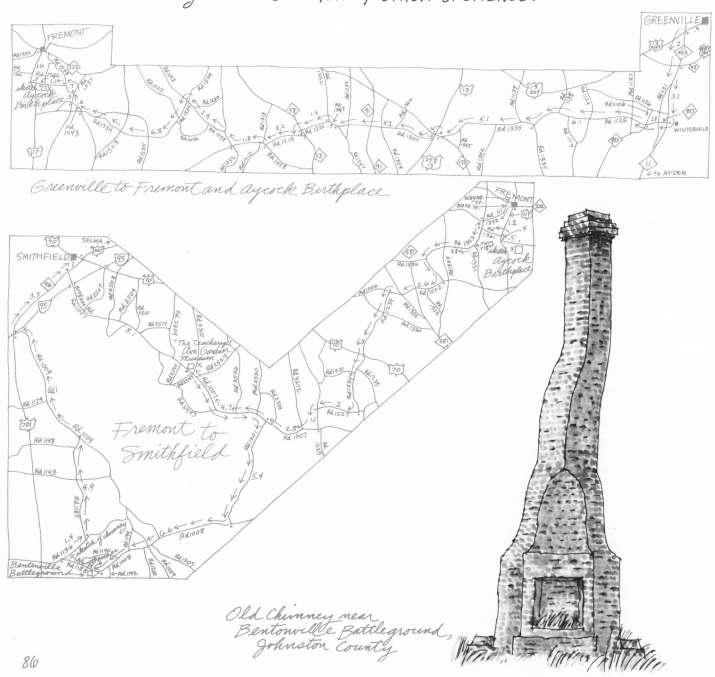

Greenville to Fremont and Aycock Birthplace

Fremont to Smithfield

Old Chimney near
Bentonville Battleground,
Johnston County

The Teacherage, Johnston County

Back roads to Raleigh from Smithfield

401 ↑ RALEIGH
(3 miles to
Interstate 40)

4.2
Rd 1010

Rd 2728
50
Holland's Church
Rd 2727

3.4
Rd 1010
Rd 1010 1.5
Rd 1010 2.1
Rd 1010
Rd 2725
Rd 2731
50
42

42

DRUG STORE (old drug store on left)

Rd 1010 8.2
Rd 1511
Rd 1330
Rd 1511
Elizabeth Church
Rd 1504

Rd 1555
4.4

70
301
70
1.1
Rd 1978
Rd 1010 1.6
210
Rd 1501
go straight on 1010
SMITHFIELD
210
96

Virginia

Back Roads to Murfreesboro

HALIFAX   MURFREESBORO

Murfreesboro
to Hope
Plantation

Elizabeth City to
Hertford, Edenton and
Hope Plantation

ELIZABETH
CITY

95

Tarboro
to
Halifax

HERTFORD

EDENTON

Kitty
Hawk

Hope
Plantation   WINDSOR

Edenton
to
Somerset Place

MANTEO

TARBORO

64

PLYMOUTH

Somerset
Place

Wilson to
Tarboro

Roads to Plymouth
and Washington

WILSON   GREENVILLE

WASHINGTON   BELHAVEN

BATH   Lake Mattamuskeet

17

The free ferries to
Oriental and
Bath

Eastern North Carolina back roads

Central North Carolina

KINSTON

Roads to New Bern   NEW
BERN

ORIENTAL

Cape
Hatteras

FAYETTEVILLE   KENANSVILLE

421

JACKSONVILLE

MAXTON   Wilmington to
Moore's Creek and
Kenansville

95

17

Atlantic Ocean

Maxton to Fair Bluff, Chadbourn,
and Lake Waccamaw

Moore's Creek
Battlefield

South Carolina

FAIR
BLUFF   CHADBOURN

Lake
Waccamaw

WILMINGTON

Orton
Plantation
and Old
Brunswick
Ruins

Eastern North Carolina

The land is sandier and whiter and has flattened out here where rivers meet sounds, bays, and the ocean.

Some of the first settlers in American history arrived here, sent from England by Sir Walter Raleigh in 1585 and in 1587. The latter group of settlers disappeared without a trace, along with Virginia Dare, the first child of English parentage born in the New World. The first permanent English residents in North Carolina migrated from Virginia settlements.

An appreciation of history can still be aroused along the routes I have chosen. I stay clear of the highways and the more developed areas, hoping to recapture my moments of reflection on North Carolina's historic past.

Wilson to Tarboro

I sigh in relief every time I leave the big highway and head off on the back roads! This is tobacco country and planting is in full swing on this day in late April.

The admirable town of Tarboro takes great pride in its history, as evidenced by the extensive restoration that has taken place. The town common remains much as it was in colonial times. In the Common I draw a 1910 fountain dedicated to the memory of Private Henry L. Wyatt Edgecombe, killed on June 10, 1861. On the right is the monument to the Confederate soldiers of Edgecombe County, "Defenders of State Sovereignty."

There is much to see in Tarboro and a good place to get full information is the Blount-Bridgers House on Bridgers Street at St. Andrews Court.

The Common, Tarboro, Edgecombe County

One of North Carolina's most beautiful graveyards is the Gothic-style Calvary Episcopal Church. The churchyard is a botanical treasure with its collection of unusual trees from all over the world. I sit in a quiet place in the dense shade to draw this angel whose features, owing to a century of erosion, are only subtly visible.

Tarboro to Halifax

Along the way to Halifax I stop at the historic town of Enfield. Here I locate the cellar home where Lafayette made a speech from the upper porch in 1824.

The town of Halifax was founded in 1760; nine years later it had a total of 60 houses and public buildings.

Young Tobacco Plant, Wilson County

North Carolina's Fourth Provincial Congress met here in 1776, as did the Fifth; and George Washington was a visitor on the sixteenth and seventeenth of April 1791. By 1830, Halifax had become the cultural center of North Carolina.

95   Rd 1001

Rd 1615

12.7

Rd 561   1216

561   Rd 1204

Rd 1207

Eden Church 1760

Rd 1206

Rd 1001

Rd 461   1618

903   125   301

☐ Visitor Center

■ HALIFAX
✗ sketch
1.0

561

Rd 1201

125

903

561

301

1.8

481   Rd 1001

.5   ■ ENFIELD

301

Rd 1100

6.9   Rd 1003

Rd 1109

Whitaker's Chapel

2.7

Rd 1100   Rd 1108

.5

Rd 1423

Rd 1429   Rd 1001

8.4

from Hwy 44 see lovely plantation home (private)

44

Rd 1422

Rd 1431

Rd 1420

.6   97

97

97

LEGGETT

2.4   Rd 1500

Rd 1501

stay right

Rd 1500

2.1   Rd 1514

Rd 1515

44

64

2.3

44

BUS 64   1.5

TARBORO
wilson St.   ✗ sketch

Detail of Enfield

west Franklin

← Rd 1001

Cellar Home (sits back from street)

North Church

Sharrod Heights

Glenview Rd.   Whitfield ←

Down town Enfield

Myrtle Lawn Plantation (private) 1816

Rd 1003

Tarboro to Halifax

angel, Calvary Church, Tarboro, Edgecombe County

93

I make a drawing of the "Clerk's Office."
Its architecture is described as "vernacular," a
combining of individual features of various styles
into a new expression. Constructed in 1832, the
brick building contains three offices separated by
solid brick walls with no interior doors. They could
be entered only from the street. Across the
street are the graves of Confederate general
Junius Daniel, editor Abraham Hodge, and U.S.
district judge John Sitgreaves, important Halifax
residents of times past.

The Clerk's Office, 1830, Halifax, Halifax County

Buckhorn Church, Como, Hertford County

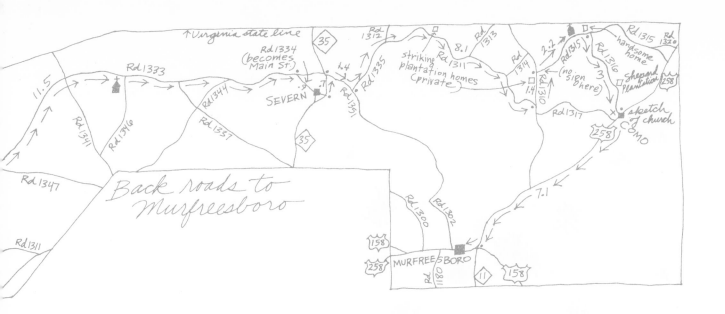

Back roads to Murfreesboro

The land is flat but interesting along these roads
past cropland and forest, plantations and simple farms.
I explore the charming town of Severn and, in Como, draw
a picture of the 1910 Buckhorn Baptist Church.
The many stately old homes in and around
Murfreesboro remind me of its colonial and antebellum
past. Murfreesboro is making a concerted effort to
keep its historic architecture from being destroyed.

I pass through the towns of Union, Fraziers Crossroads, Poor Town, Hexlena, and Rhodes along these secondary roads.

Stately trees shade the small community of Republican.

Arriving at Hope Plantation I discover I am the only visitor. I am given a very informative tour after which I settle down in the old winter kitchen to sketch several implements of the early 1800s. In my drawing you can see a revolving fireplace toaster, a candleholder, a wick trimmer (the pointed end pried the candle from its holder), and a goffering iron (used for crimping or fluting ruffled shirts).

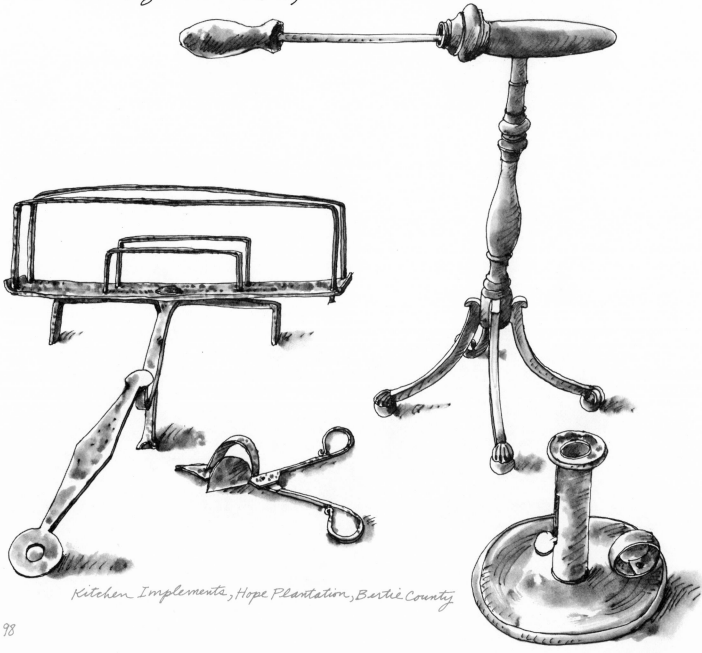

Kitchen Implements, Hope Plantation, Bertie County

David Stone built
this impressive house about
1800. He was an important
man, having served as a
governor of North
Carolina and as a United
States senator. A section
of plaster wall was discovered
in his library with a clearly
discernible penciled
message he had written
following his beloved
wife's death. I copy its
sweet sentiment for
you to see.

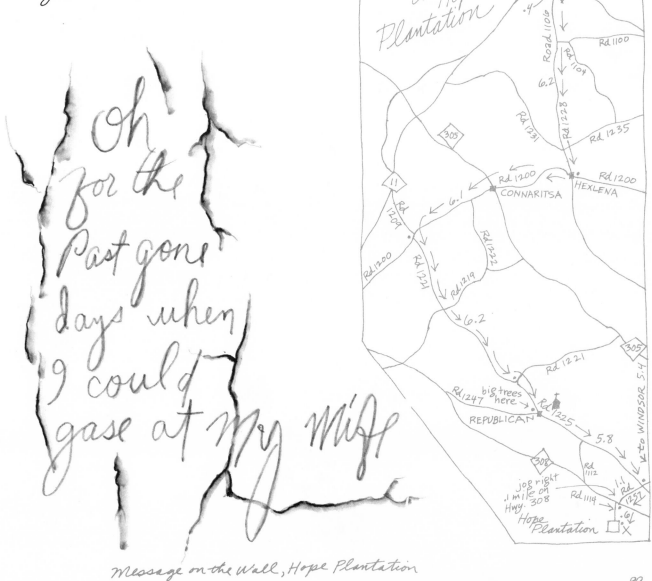

Oh
for the
Past gone
days when
I could
gase at my wife

Message on the Wall, Hope Plantation

Elizabeth City to Hertford, Edenton, and Hope Plantation

The Museum of the Albemarle is here in Elizabeth City; the historic district covers 30 blocks in the heart of town.

Elizabeth City to Hertford and Edenton

Newbold-White House, 1685, Perquimans County

Near Hertford on my back road tour is the 17th-century Newbold-White House. Early settler Joseph Scott supposedly built the brick house in 1685. It has had some 30 occupants since then, including farmers, carpenters, a mariner, and a congressman. I draw the sturdy structure, impressed by its simplicity and picturesque location:

At Edenton I draw one of North Carolina's most frequently pictured historic scenes, the Barker House on Albemarle Sound. To the left are the "Dram Trees" where sailors cooled their rum in colonial times.

Barker House, now the Visitor Center for Edenton, was built in 1782. Penelope Barker, who married three times, had each husband buy her house before their marriage so that she would have her own cash on hand. In those days, a wife was required to relinquish all her familial possessions to her husband's family after his death. It is said that Penelope organized the famous Edenton Tea Party in 1774 at which time the ladies of Edenton signed a declaration resolving "not to drink any more tea, nor wear any more British cloth, uniting with their husbands in opposing the oppressions of the English crown."

Barker House, Edenton, Chowan County

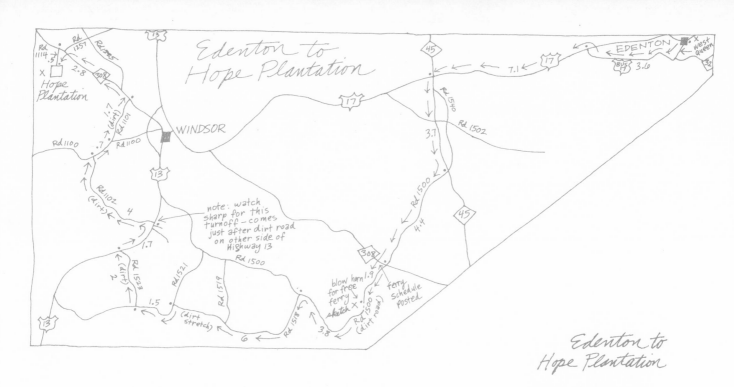

Edenton to
Hope Plantation

(map labels:) Edenton to Hope Plantation · Rd 1114 · Rd 1257 · Rd 1065 · 13 · 45 · EDENTON · West Queen · 17 · BUS · 3.6 · 2.8 · 308 · Hope Plantation · X · 7.1 · 1.7 · (dirt) · Rd 1101 · WINDSOR · 17 · Rd 1540 · Rd 1502 · 3.7 · Rd 1100 · .7 · Rd 1100 · Rd 1500 · 13 · Rd 1102 (dirt) · 4 · note: watch sharp for this turnoff—comes just after dirt road on other side of Highway 13 · 308 · 45 · 4.4 · 1.7 · Rd 1523 (dirt) · 2 · Rd 1521 · Rd 1500 · blow horn 1.9 for free ferry · sketch · X · ferry schedule posted · Rd 1500 (dirt road) · 1.5 · (dirt stretch) · Rd 1519 · Rd 1518 · 3.8 · 13 · 6

Edenton to
Hope Plantation

Back roads go
past forest and
meadows of yellow wildflowers where black cows graze.
There are long vistas of cropland with cornfields ready for
plowing. Snapping turtles, looking like domed rocks in the
road, suck in their heads and tails as my car straddles them.

104   Ferry across the Cashie, Bertie County

After sketching a bit at the Cashie River ferry crossing, I toot my horn to let the captain know I am ready. He jumps aboard, starts the engine, and chugs over to my side of the stream. There is even a quiet picnic spot at this old river crossing. I suddenly hope that a bridge is never built.

Edenton to Somerset Place

After crossing Albemarle Sound, country roads proceed to the pleasant town of Creswell. At Somerset Place, built in 1830, I draw the plantation house from the old carriage road. Tall bald cypresses are an impressive part of the landscape. I sit in the shade of a tree. It had rained earlier and a breeze periodically shakes droplets from the still-wet leaves onto me. Gnats and mosquitoes seek me out. Huge black bees slowly buzz by and a jet black snake slides past.

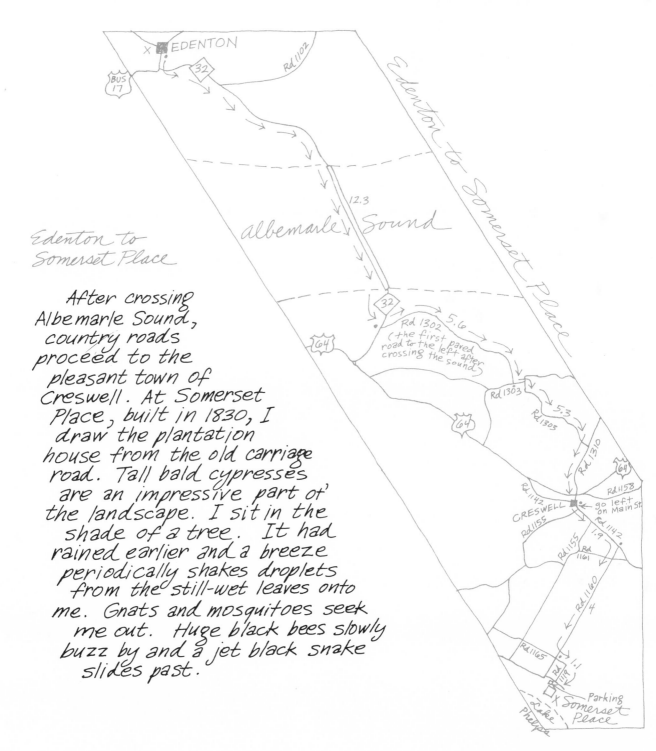

Somerset Place, Washington County

Perhaps the haunting atmosphere of this place is best expressed in a written message from Charles Pettigrew to John Leigh in June 1790: "I sit under the shade of three beautiful Holleys. The surrounding scene is truly romantic . . . the prospect toward the water is very beautiful and extensive, while the gentle breezes play over the surface of the crystal fluid . . . On three angles of the improvement, ye woods are luxuriantly tall, & dressed in a foliage of the deepest verdure, while the cultivated field exhibits the utmost power of vegetative nature, and arrests my eye from every other object."

Trees form a canopy over Road 1164.

Plymouth is strategically located along the Roanoke River and is a historic town worth exploring.

Washington has the distinction of being the first town in the United States to bear that name. It was changed from "Forks of the Tar" in 1776. A walking tour views some 23 sites of historic and architectural significance.

Roads to Plymouth and Washington

PLYMOUTH
x large lumber plant
E. Main St
1.8
3.6 W. Main
64
149
64
turn right at "Y"
64
5.6
32
.9 ROPER
left on 1122 (Buncombe Ave.) into Roper
11.9
CRESWELL
Rd 1149
Rd 1126
Rd 1164
2.4
Rd 1160
Rd 1183
Rd 1106 .4
x
Somerset Place
Lake Phelps

Road 1100
64
Rd. 1106
32
18.2
Rd 1508
Rd 1529
Rd 1532
Rd 1528
2.3
Rd 1507
.8
Rd 1525
Rd 1526
32
dirt
32

WASHINGTON
171
8.1
1.1
US 264
Rd 1501 (Highland Drive)
WASHINGTON PARK
32
264

bridge
West Main Street
32
WASHINGTON
see the houses along West Main and Stewart Parkway
Middle Fork Railroad engine "Ole No. 7"
Edgewater Drive
Washington Park community
Isabella Ave.
Walnut Street
Detail showing a drive through the exceptional Washington Park Community
Riverside Drive

Tobacco Field with Snapping Turtle, Robeson County

Maxton to Fair Bluff, Chadbourn, and Lake Waccamaw

This is sandy, flat land broken by fringes of forest. Swamps are crossed or paralleled on this journey through tobacco and corn country. I draw several farm scenes that include the old tobacco barns. Today they are used chiefly to house equipment and for general storage as larger and more efficient enclosures elsewhere serve for curing the tobacco. In earlier times tobacco leaves were gathered from the fields as they ripened and hung under the eaves of the barn. The fields would be picked over from three to ten times at intervals of a week or ten days. Later the leaves were hung on four-foot sticks arranged in tiers for curing in the barn.

Tobacco Barn Landscape, Robeson County

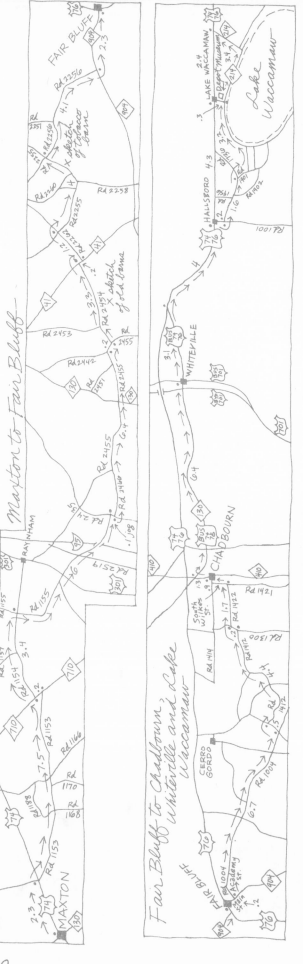

At Fair Bluff the
Lumber River flows by,
bordered by old homes
and old oaks laden with
Spanish moss.
    In Chadbourn a
Strawberry Festival is in
progress, commemorating
the beginning of straw-
berry culture there in
1895. Since 1926 a dance
and a parade have been
held every year as part
of the festival.
Chadbourn signals the
importance of straw-
berries in this area by
picturing them on its
street signs.
    An interesting side
trip off Highways 74
and 76 goes by egg-
shaped Lake Waccamaw
and the Lake Waccamaw
Depot Museum.

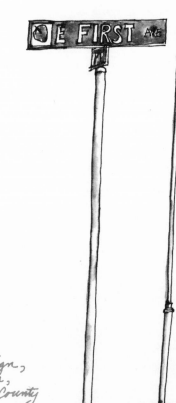

E FIRST AVE

Street Sign,
Chadbourn,
Columbus County

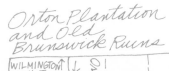

Colonial Food Cooler

Orton Plantation and Old Brunswick Ruins

A short secondary road off Highway 133 takes me to the entrance of Orton Plantation Gardens.

A walk through the gardens gives me time to soak up the southern antebellum atmosphere of this old rice plantation. There is a view of the fields where once superior quality rice was grown. The land is now leased to the North Carolina Wildlife Resources Commission for a waterfowl refuge.

The ruins of Brunswick Town are nearby and I draw several items excavated there and now displayed at the Visitor Center. William Dry of Brunswick was able to chill his wine to the proper temperature by lowering this cooling device into a well in his cellar dairy room.

Curlers were wound with hair and baked inside a loaf of bread to set curls for sewing onto gentlemen's wigs.

The rise and fall of Brunswick Town is a fascinating subject. It was settled in 1726, but by 1830 the place was a total ruin. The British burned it in 1776; malaria-carrying mosquitoes, destructive hurricanes, and high humidity finally finished it off. In 1842 the site was sold to Orton Plantation for $4.25.

Orton Plantation and Old Brunswick Ruins

WILMINGTON 14.5
133
Rd. 1529
.6
Rd. 1530
133
SOUTHPORT 12.8
Orton Pond
2.7
Orton Plantation
Old Brunswick Ruins
Cape Fear River

Colonial Wig Curler

111

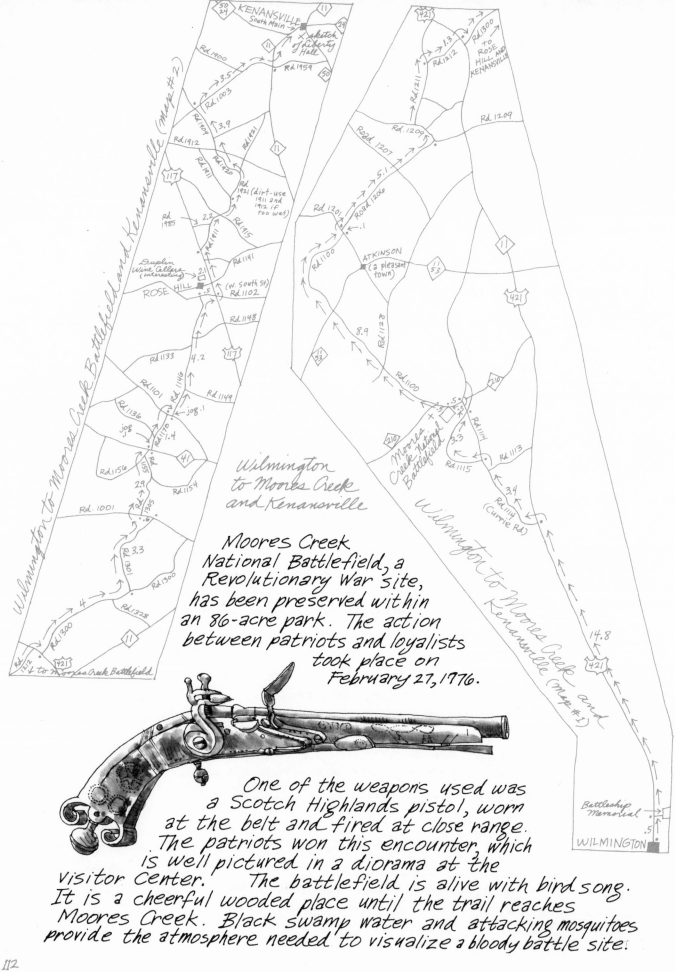

KENANSVILLE
South Main

x sketch
of Liberty
Hall

Rd. 1900

Rd. 1959

Rd. 1003

Rd. 1921 (dirt-use
1911 and
1912 if
too wet)

Rd 1912

Rd 1420

Rd 1911

Rd 1985

Rd 1915

Duplin
Wine Cellars
(interesting)

Rd. 1141

ROSE HILL

(w. South St.)
Rd. 1102

Rd. 1148

Rd. 1133

Rd. 1101

Rd. 1149

Rd. 1149

Rd. 1136

jog .1

jog .1

Rd. 1170

Rd. 1156

Rd. 1154

Rd. 1001

Rd. 1305

Rd. 1301

Rd. 1328

Rd. 1300

Rd. 1712
to Moores Creek Battlefield

Wilmington to Moores Creek Battlefield and Kenansville (Map #2)

to
ROSE
HILL AND
KENANSVILLE

Rd. 1300

Rd. 1211

Rd. 1212

Rd. 1209

Road 1207

Rd. 1209

Rd. 1201

Road 1206

Rd. 1100

ATKINSON
(a pleasant
town)

Rd. 1128

Rd. 1100

Moores Creek National Battlefield

Rd. 1114

Rd. 1113

Rd. 1115

Rd. 1114
(Currie Rd.)

Wilmington to Moores Creek and Kenansville (Map #1)

Battleship
Memorial

WILMINGTON

*Wilmington
to Moores Creek
and Kenansville*

Moores Creek
National Battlefield, a
Revolutionary War site,
has been preserved within
an 86-acre park. The action
between patriots and loyalists
took place on
February 27, 1776.

One of the weapons used was
a Scotch Highlands pistol, worn
at the belt and fired at close range.
The patriots won this encounter, which
is well pictured in a diorama at the
visitor center. The battlefield is alive with bird song.
It is a cheerful wooded place until the trail reaches
Moores Creek. Black swamp water and attacking mosquitoes
provide the atmosphere needed to visualize a bloody battle site.

Back roads lead me to Kenansville where I visit and sketch Liberty Hall. It was given that name by James Kenan because of the many political meetings held there in the late 1700s.

Liberty Hall is a prime example of Greek Revival architecture. Its eleven rooms and two T-shaped halls are tastefully furnished and include as well some original Kenan family possessions. One of the windows bears a discreetly scratched message from Emily Howard Kenan: "Tell me not, in mournful numbers, Life is but an empty dream, Feb. 18, 1899." The words are Longfellow's. Beneath the kitchen is a large wine cellar. Many "dependencies" are out back, including a smokehouse, chicken house, and bathhouse.

113

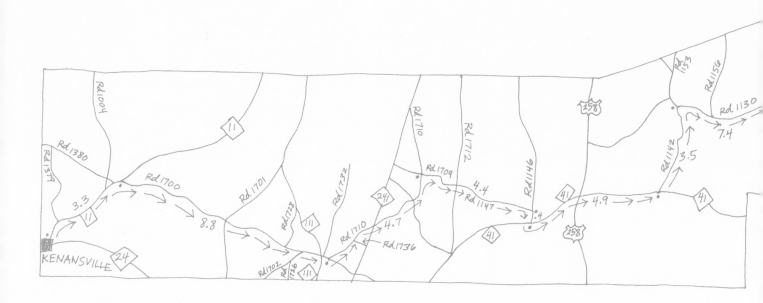

Landscape near Trenton, Jones County

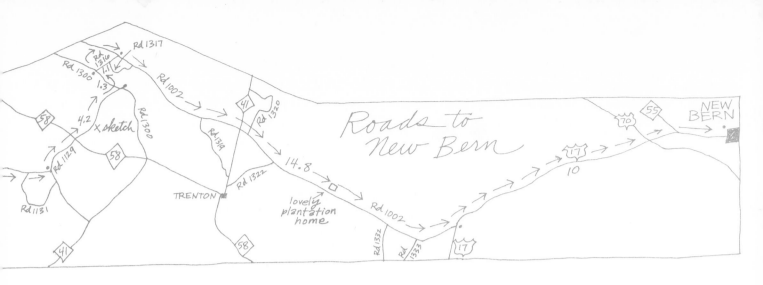

Roads to
New Bern

TRENTON

lovely
plantation
home

NEW
BERN

Roads to New Bern

The gently rolling land is of sandy soil. I see pigpens,
chicken houses, old farms, and old barns fringed by forest.
In my drawing, on the left, is the deserted 1860s house
once owned by Archie Eubanks. A young farm boy watching
me draw says that pigs had been penned right up to the
house. "It's in pretty bad shape," he tells me. Soybeans
are to be planted around the old tobacco barns on the
right. "I've got to cut ground," he says. Some of last
year's tobacco leaves are bound and given to me by the
boy's father. I carry them in my car for a long time,
enjoying their sweet smell.
    At New Bern is the Fireman's
Museum and the incredible
Tryon Palace and much
more to see.

115

The Emmett Winslow, Craven County

The free ferries to Oriental and Bath

　　The "Governor Cherry" takes me across the Neuse River. I sketch the "Emmett Winslow," gulls crying loudly and hoping for handouts off the stern. I draw boats in the quiet, quaint town of Oriental where Smith, Kershaw, and Greens creeks form an inlet off the Neuse.

Scene in Oriental, Pamlico County

Another free ferry crosses Pamlico River and the road leads to Bath, North Carolina's oldest town, founded in 1706. Some of the original, significant structures have survived here, including St. Thomas Church. It is lightly raining while I draw the entrance to St. Thomas, and I juggle umbrella and drawing pad. A young gentleman is pleased that I have recorded the name "Thomas Boyd", which is to the left of the door. He says he is a descendant! Of Boyd, the stone tablet says, "He was an honest man. The sweet remembrance of the just / Shall flourish when he sleeps in dust."

I follow roads to Belhaven where the incredibly diverse collection of the late Eva Blount Way is on view at Belhaven Memorial Museum.

On my way to Roanoke Island and Cape Hatteras I travel my last North Carolina back road along the north shore of Lake Mattamuskeet.

St. Thomas Church,
Bath, Beaufort County

118

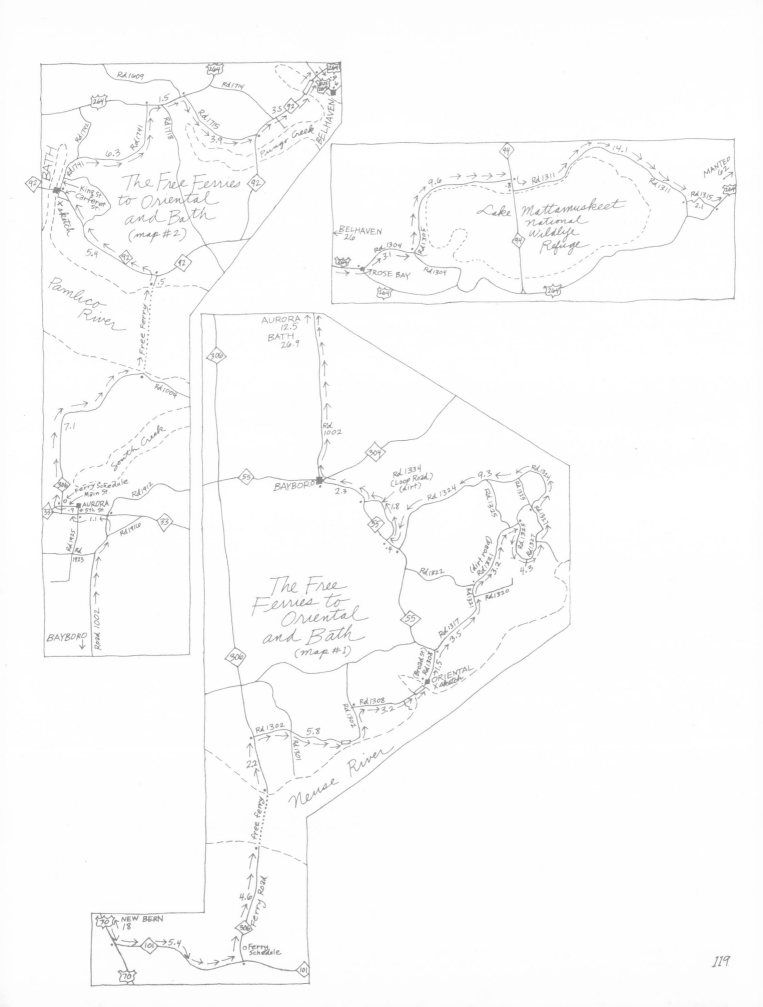

Rd 1609   Rd 1714   264

264   1.5   Rd 1715   BUS 264   264

Rd 1741   Rd 1718   Rd 1715   3.5   92   BELHAVEN

Rd 1742   6.3   Rd 1741   3.9   Punzo Creek

92   BATH   Rd 1741   King St.   92   92

Carteret St.   The Free Ferries   92

X sketch   to Oriental   94   14.1

5.4   92   and Bath   MANTEO

92   (map #2)   9.6   Rd 1311   62

.5   .8   Rd 1311   Rd 1315   264

Pamlico River   Lake Mattamuskeet   2.1

Free Ferry   National   Rd 1305

Wildlife

306   BELHAVEN   Refuge

Rd 1004   26   Rd 1304   264

South Creek   264   ROSE BAY   Rd 1304   264

7.1   3.1

AURORA   264

Ferry Schedule   12.5

306   Main St.   BATH

33   Rd 1912   26.9

.9   AURORA   Rd   BAYBORO

33   5th St.   1002   Rd 1334   9.3   Rd 1324

1.1   Rd 1910   304   (Loop Road)   Rd 1324

Rd 1925   (dirt)   Rd 1325   Rd 1321

Rd   55   1.8   Rd 1325

1925   BAYBORO   Rd 1327

2.3   55   Rd 1325

Road 1002   (dirt road)   Rd 1327

BAYBORO   .4   Rd 1321   3.2   4.3

Rd 1322   Rd 1321   Rd 1320

The Free   55   Rd 1317

Ferries to   Rd 1317   3.5

Oriental

and Bath   (Broad St.)   ORIENTAL

(map #1)   Rd 1308   1.5   X sketch

306   Rd 1308   Rd 1308

Rd 1302   Rd 1308   Rd 1308   3.2

5.8   Rd 1301   Rd 1302

Rd 1302   Neuse River

2.2

Free ferry

Ferry Road   4.6

70   NEW BERN

18   306   o Ferry Schedule

101   5.4

70   101

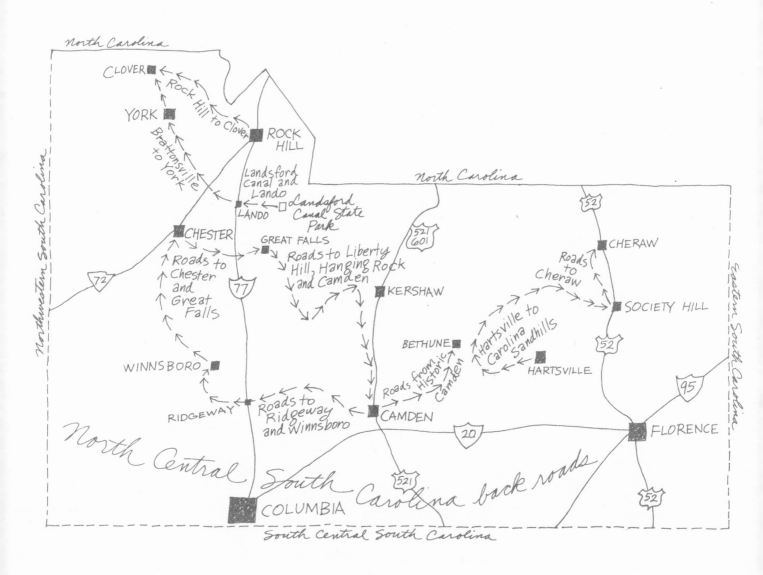

North Carolina

CLOVER

Rock Hill to Clover

YORK

Brattonsville to York

Northwestern South Carolina

ROCK HILL

Landsford Canal and Lando

LANDO

☐ Landsford Canal State Park

North Carolina

CHESTER

GREAT FALLS

Roads to Liberty Hill, Hanging Rock and Camden

Roads to Chester and Great Falls

72

77

521 601

CHERAW

Roads to Cheraw

52

SOCIETY HILL

KERSHAW

Hartsville to Carolina Sandhills

52

BETHUNE

HARTSVILLE

Roads from Historic Camden

WINNSBORO

RIDGEWAY

Roads to Ridgeway and Winnsboro

CAMDEN

95

20

FLORENCE

Eastern South Carolina

North Central South Carolina back roads

521

COLUMBIA

52

South Central South Carolina

120

azaleas

North Central South Carolina

I drive the lesser roads and the byways to
enjoy this good land. I yearn to see it, smell
it, listen to it—to enjoy South Carolina to the
fullest each day I spend here. I have no
desire to hurry as I leave the rest of the
world behind me and seek out the
back roads. Come with me!

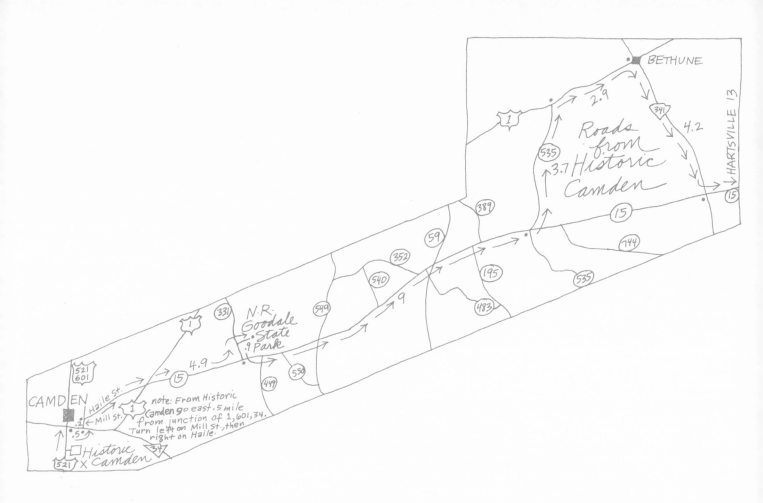

BETHUNE

HARTSVILLE 13

1

341

2.9

Roads from Historic Camden

535

4.2

3.7

389

HARTSVILLE

15

15

59

744

352

540

195

535

9

549

483

331

N.R. Goodale State .9 Park

1

4.9

521 601

15

550

Haile St.

449

CAMDEN

Mill St.

1

.2

note: From Historic Camden go east .5 mile from junction of 1, 601, 34. Turn left on Mill St., then right on Haile.

.5

Historic Camden

34

521

X

Camden itself has over 60 homes and buildings specially noted by the Kershaw County Historical Society. Just south of the main town are the remains of the old town, its six small surrounding forts and a number of old structures including the carefully reconstructed Kershaw-Cornwallis House. Once a year here at Historic Camden, the citizens, dressed as Revolutionary War characters, reenact the events of 1781. That was the year Nathanael Greene and his men drove the British from Camden by inflicting particularly heavy losses upon them at the battle of Hobkirks Hill.

I stop to picnic at N. R. Goodale State Park, then continue on to Bethune, the egg laying capital of South Carolina and home of the annual "Chicken Strut" celebration. It is spring and dogwood is blooming up and down every street. Such floral beauty lifts the spirits and pleases the eye.

Kershaw House, Historic Camden, Kershaw County

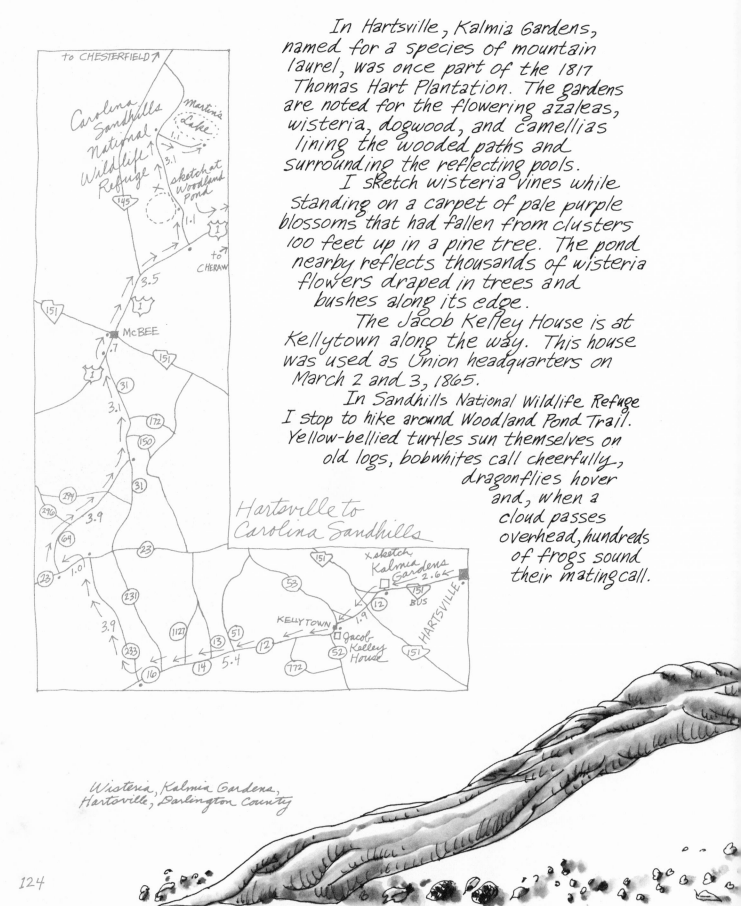

In Hartsville, Kalmia Gardens, named for a species of mountain laurel, was once part of the 1817 Thomas Hart Plantation. The gardens are noted for the flowering azaleas, wisteria, dogwood, and camellias lining the wooded paths and surrounding the reflecting pools.

I sketch wisteria vines while standing on a carpet of pale purple blossoms that had fallen from clusters 100 feet up in a pine tree. The pond nearby reflects thousands of wisteria flowers draped in trees and bushes along its edge.

The Jacob Kelley House is at Kellytown along the way. This house was used as Union headquarters on March 2 and 3, 1865.

In Sandhills National Wildlife Refuge I stop to hike around Woodland Pond Trail. Yellow-bellied turtles sun themselves on old logs, bobwhites call cheerfully, dragonflies hover and, when a cloud passes overhead, hundreds of frogs sound their mating call.

Wisteria, Kalmia Gardens, Hartsville, Darlington County

124

Woodland Pond, Chesterfield County

I walk quietly and cautiously along the path to sketch the turtles and manage to draw ten of them before they plunge into the water to swim to a more distant log.

The fishing season has begun and largemouth bass are the target for the fishermen here at Woodland Pond.

Roads to Cheraw

I visit the quaint little town of Society Hill, established in 1736. Old homes and stores have been nicely restored.

On the way to Cheraw I stop at Cheraw National Fish Hatchery where several million largemouth bass, redear sunfish, bluegill, and channel catfish are hatched and distributed every year. There is a small aquarium and a chance to see yellow-bellied turtles at close range.

I drive through Cheraw State Park, the oldest and largest in the state park system of South Carolina.

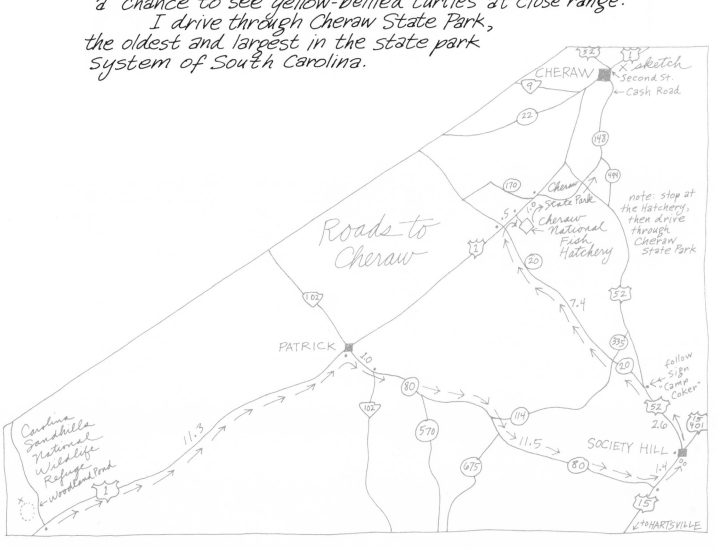

In Cheraw is old St. David's Episcopal Church (1770), the last church built in South Carolina under the authority of King George III. A long freight train is passing adjacent to the graveyard where I sit drawing, its whistle drowning out the calls of the mockingbirds. In this cemetery lie soldiers of every war, including the American Revolution. Many of the king's 71st Highlanders died on this site in 1780 and were buried in a mass grave near the church doors.

Along Third Street great old houses, flowers, grass and trees create a parklike atmosphere. Lafayette House is at 235 Third Street, where in 1825 a reception was held for the celebrated general.

Old St. David's, Cheraw, Chesterfield County

129

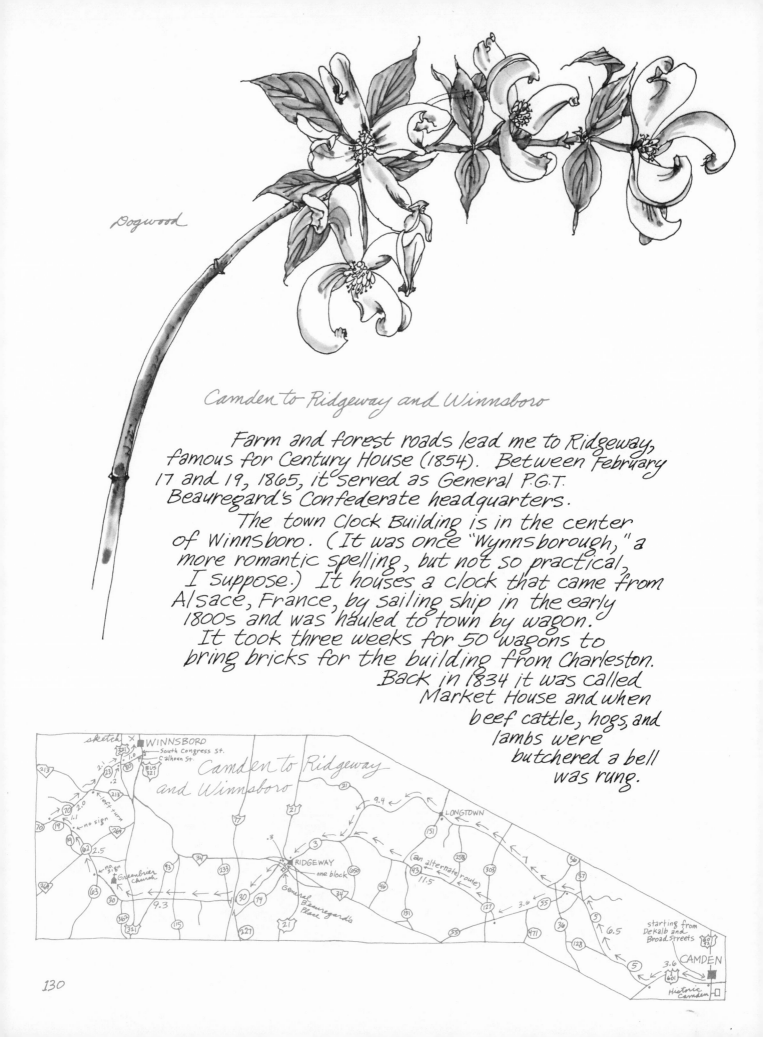

Dogwood

Camden to Ridgeway and Winnsboro

Farm and forest roads lead me to Ridgeway, famous for Century House (1854). Between February 17 and 19, 1865, it served as General P.G.T. Beauregard's Confederate headquarters.

The town Clock Building is in the center of Winnsboro. (It was once "Wynnsborough," a more romantic spelling, but not so practical, I suppose.) It houses a clock that came from Alsace, France, by sailing ship in the early 1800s and was hauled to town by wagon.

It took three weeks for 50 wagons to bring bricks for the building from Charleston.

Back in 1834 it was called Market House and when beef cattle, hogs, and lambs were butchered a bell was rung.

Everyone, as well as all the dogs for miles around, knew that fresh meat was then available.

The 1823 courthouse nearby was designed by Robert Mills. Lord Cornwallis is credited with naming Fairfield County, of which Winnsboro is the county seat. According to one story, when he was headquartered here in 1780 he kept repeating the comment, "What fair fields are these." So be it.

Winnsboro Clock Tower, Fairfield County

Roads to Chester
and Great Falls

To reach Chester I go through much forestland with occasional views of farms and plantation houses. Chester's downtown has turn-of-the century buildings, winding hilly streets, and the famous Aaron Burr Rock, mounted in perpetuity in front of 103 Main Street. The rock gained its fame through an incident that occurred in 1887 when Burr passed through town under guard on his way to Virginia to be tried for treason.

IN 1806
AARAN BURR WHILE PASSING
THROUGH CHESTER, A PRISONER,
DISMOUNTED ON THIS ROCK AND
APPEALED, IN VAIN, TO THE
CITIZENS FOR HELP

The former vice president suddenly shook off his guards, mounted the rock and appealed for help from the local citizenry. He was instantly seized, and the next day he and his custodians proceeded to Richmond.
A wild turkey is spied on back roads to Great Falls!

Aaron Burr Rock, Chester

132

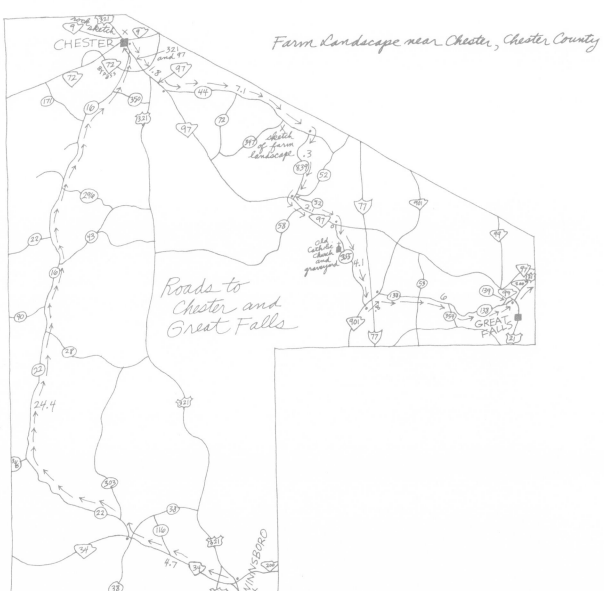

Farm Landscape near Chester, Chester County

Roads to
Chester and
Great Falls

CHESTER

WINNSBORO

GREAT FALLS

Old Catholic church and graveyard

sketch of farm landscape

rock sketch

134 Liberty Hill church, Kershaw County

Roads to Liberty Hill, Hanging Rock, and Camden

At the charming community of Liberty Hill I draw an elegant church. The congregation has slipped to 98, I am told, not large enough to support a full-time minister. I notice that bees have built a hive in the steeple. The decorative cemetery gate came from a mansion that had burned down in the late 1800s. The stone posts supporting the gate came from a local quarry. Some cost $5 apiece then, others merely 50¢.

Back on the road again I locate Hanging
Rock Battle Site. On August 6, 1870, General
Thomas Sumter and Major William B. Davie and
their militiamen defeated a British force
twice their size at this place of many trees
and huge balanced rocks.

Hanging Rock Monument detail →

markers
dirt road
too steep

Hanging Rock Battle Monument

Roads to Liberty Hill, Hanging Rock and Camden

GREAT FALLS

Cedar Springs Rd.

Green Rd.

LIBERTY HILL

Stoneboro Rd.

X sketch Liberty Hill Church

John Hale Rd.

handsome mansion

Truesdale Road

Maybloom Gully

Flat Rock Road

Hanging Rock Rd.

Baron de Kalb monument....
site of Battle of Camden
August 16, 1780

CAMDEN

Hanging Rock Battle Site, Kershaw County

Landsford Canal, Chester County

Landsford Canal and Lando

    I stop to draw a snapping turtle. It has a clump
of mud on its back, having just crawled from a mudhole
at the side of the road. Its teeth and claws are long
and sharp and it can manipulate them quite quickly
when threatened.

Lying on my stomach in the road I draw the turtle at eye level.

An inchworm crawls across my drawing paper, but I am too intent on completing my work to bother removing it. The turtle eyes me all the while, at the ready should I move closer. I don't. I finish my sketch and continue my way to Landsford Canal State Park.

It is an enjoyable 2-mile walk alongside the canal. The great granite blocks that once formed its locks are still in place. The main canal itself is simply a channel dug out of the earth. It was built in the 1820s to make navigation possible past the rapids of the Catawba River.

I travel to the little town of Lando, where in August there will be a celebration of early mill life.

Snapping Turtle

Brattonsville to York

      One of South Carolina's outstanding living history
complexes is at Brattonsville. There are three
distinctive houses, a general store, and a number
of outbuildings, including a brick slave cabin.
      I arrive the day after a devastating tornado
has swept through the Carolinas. Three chain saws

Cleanup Time at Brattonsville, York County

buzz as volunteers clean up the damage from the great rain and windstorm that accompanied the tornado. The Homestead stands tall, however, as it has since 1828 when it was completed. It is a good Piedmont—South Carolina interpretation of Federal-style architecture.

142   House on North Congress Street, York, York County

In York, at 109 North Congress Street,
I sketch an old mansion said to have
been considered as a location for the
movie "Gone With the Wind." Magnolia
trees all but obscure its facade.
York city has a rich architectural
heritage and boasts one of the
largest historic districts in
the United States.

to Kings Mountain State Park

on 161 or Clover 64
on 321

5 BUS
321

x sketch
321 YORK to
ROCK
BUS HILL
321 161

35 740

Brattonsville
to
York

10 321

7.2

32

168

321 167

322

2.4

321
McCONNELLS 165
Brattonsville
sketch x 580

After contemplating the beauty of Glencairn Garden in Rock Hill I travel roads to the Museum of York and then on to Clover.

Along Faulkner Road I draw a farm landscape. Later I knock on the door of the farmhouse I have drawn and a tall old man with intense light blue eyes answers.

It is Jim Faulkner himself. I show him my drawing and when I ask how long he has lived here, he answers, "Ninety-two years—all my life." He then kindly shows me through the house he has lived in for so long. It is neatly painted and well furnished. Three sons and a daughter are in his immediate family and most live nearby. One son lives in the house shown on the right in my picture. I leave, thinking how memorable it is for a stranger to be greeted in such friendly fashion along these back roads of South Carolina.

Faulkner Ranch, York County

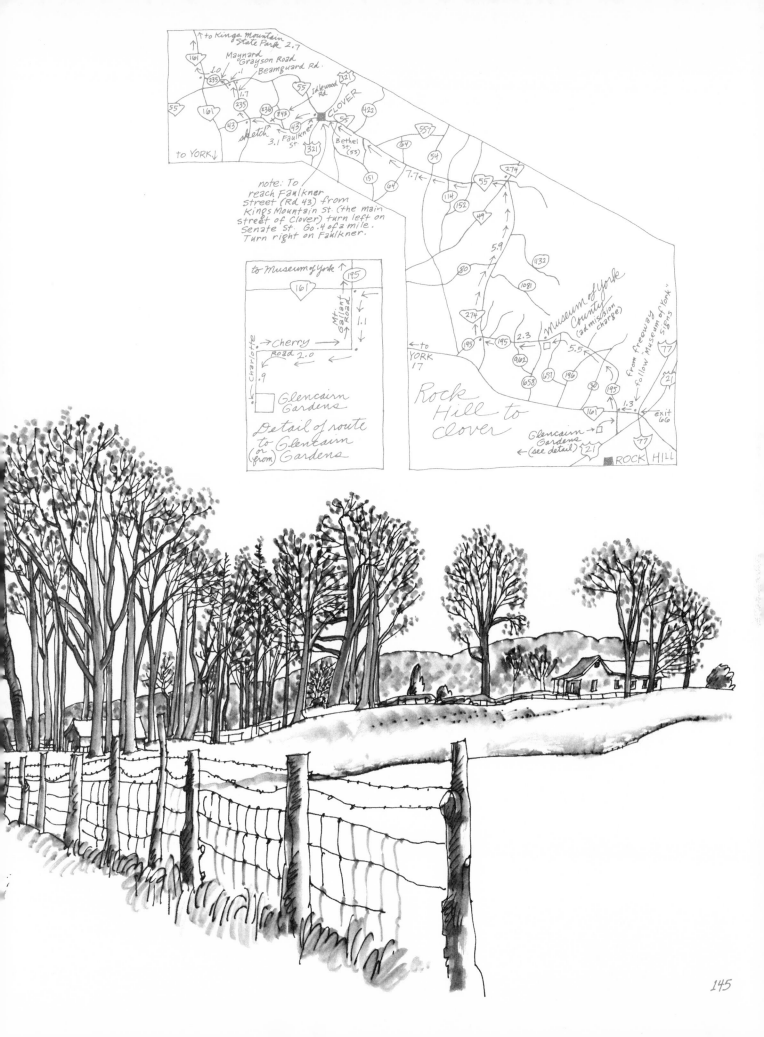

↑ to Kings Mountain State Park 2.7

161

Maynard
Grayson Road
Beamguard Rd.
1.0
235 .1
1.7
55 Idlewood Rd. 321
55 161 235 236 843 43 422 CLOVER
43 43 55
sketch→ Faulkner 321 Bethel St. (55)
to YORK↓ 3.1 St.
557
64 54
151 7.7← 55 274
64 114 55
152
49
5.9
80 1132
1081
274
195 2.3 Museum of York County (admission charge) 77
← to YORK 17 195 962 5.5
658 651 196 30 21
195
161 1.3 exit 66
Rock Hill to Clover
Glencairn Gardens (see detail) ← 21 77
ROCK HILL

note: To reach Faulkner Street (Rd 43) from Kings Mountain St. (the main street of Clover) turn left on Senate St. Go .4 of a mile. Turn right on Faulkner.

to Museum of York ↑ 195
161
Mt. Gallant Road 1.1
→ Cherry Road 2.0
Charlotte ← ·
.9
Glencairn Gardens

Detail of route to (on from) Glencairn Gardens

145

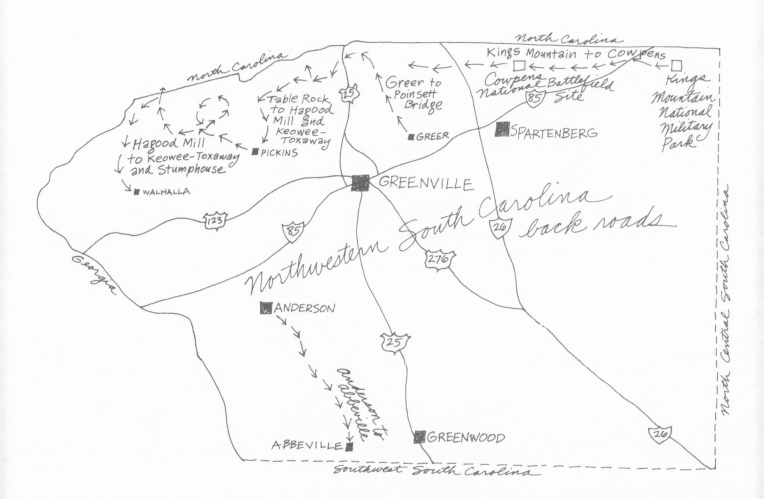

Northwestern South Carolina back roads

North Carolina
Kings Mountain to Cowpens

Cowpens National Battlefield Site

Kings Mountain National Military Park

SPARTENBERG

Greer to Poinsett Bridge

GREER

north Carolina

Table Rock to Hagood Mill and Keowee-Toxaway

Hagood Mill to Keowee-Toxaway and Stumphouse

PICKINS

WALHALLA

GREENVILLE

123

85

Georgia

ANDERSON

anderson to abbeville

ABBEVILLE

GREENWOOD

26

276

25

25

26

North Central South Carolina

Southwest South Carolina

Flame Azalea

Northwestern South Carolina

More battles and skirmishes of the
Revolutionary War were fought in South
Carolina than in any other state. Along
these roads I feel in touch with those
important events in America's early history.
Some areas seem unchanged, and I am
thankful when venerable structures have
been preserved.

Dogwood

Kings Mountain to Cowpens

I hike the Battlefield Trail at Kings Mountain National Military Park. The paved pathway goes up, down, and around the battle site where the "over-mountain" men, Carolinians and Virginians, 1000 strong, surrounded British major Patrick Ferguson and his Loyalists. When the fight was over Ferguson was dead and so were 224 others. There were 163 wounded and 716 taken prisoner.

Back roads bring me to Highway 29 and Gaffney, where I can travel the Cherokee Foothills Scenic Highway to Cowpens National Battlefield.

On January 17, 1781, Daniel Morgan, frontiersman, proved to be one of the best field tacticians of the Revolution. Here at Hannah's Cowpens, a frontier pasturing ground, Morgan, with a militia of 900 tough Continentals and backwoodsmen, beat a larger force of British regulars. In the battle 110 British died, 200 were wounded, and 500 were captured. Morgan lost only 12 men and 60 were wounded.

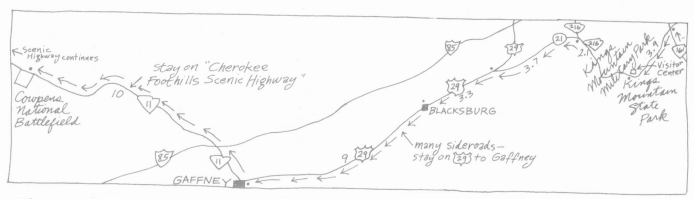

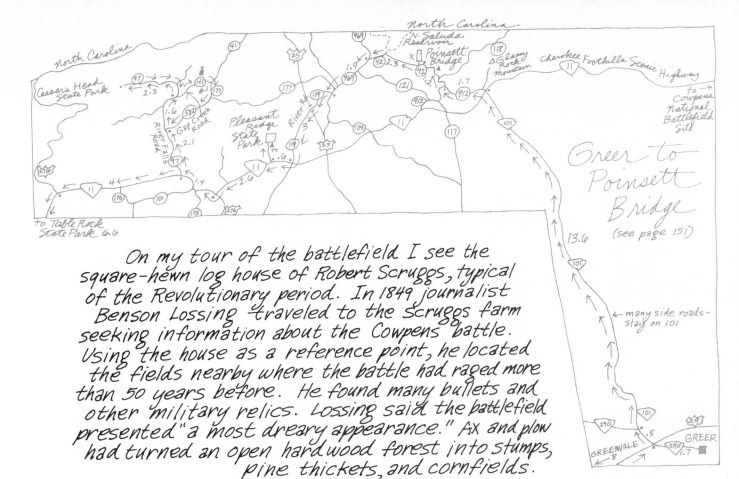

Greer to Poinsett Bridge (see page 151)

On my tour of the battlefield I see the square-hewn log house of Robert Scruggs, typical of the Revolutionary period. In 1849 journalist Benson Lossing traveled to the Scruggs farm seeking information about the Cowpens battle. Using the house as a reference point, he located the fields nearby where the battle had raged more than 50 years before. He found many bullets and other military relics. Lossing said the battlefield presented "a most dreary appearance." Ax and plow had turned an open hardwood forest into stumps, pine thickets, and cornfields.

Scruggs House, Cowpens National Battlefield, Cherokee County

149

150

Poinsett Bridge, Greenville County

Greer to Poinsett Bridge (map, page 149)

From Greer the scenery along the road through the rolling foothills is pleasantly varied. At the junction of 101 and Cherokee Foothills Scenic Highway is a fine view of Glassy Rock Mountain, 1000 feet of sheer rock face.

An old stone marker at Poinsett Bridge reads, "This bridge on the state road from Greenville to Asheville was built in 1820 by Abram Blanding, acting Commissioner, Board of Public Works, Joel R. Poinsett, President."

A stream rushes down Old Indian Mountain and over the smooth, slippery rocks here at the aging Poinsett stone bridge. Trees have barely begun to leaf. Only the sound of water tumbling over rock can be heard.

Table Rock to
Hagood Mill

Table Rock
State Park   ✗ sketch
                3.6

look sharp
for left turn
"Bob's Place"
on corner

Hickory
Hollow Rd.

sketch 5
✗ 100

Estatoe
Community
Road

Sunset
Community
Rd.

go left on
143

Hidden Valley Rd.

Midway Rd.

Sunset
Community Rd.

Mountain Grove Rd.

(dead end)

Cherokee Foothills
Scenic Hwy.

Keowee-
Toxaway
State
Park

Hagood
Mill

Hagood
Mill Rd.

Table Rock to
Hagood Mill

Prior to the Hopewell
Treaty of 1785, all of what is
now Table Rock State Park
was part of the Lower
Cherokee Nation. The Indians
called the area Sah-ka-na-ga,
the Great Blue Hills of God,
believing that the
blue haze was
the shadow of
the great spirit.
Soft, gray-
colored cliffs
drop to meet the
spring green foliage
of trees and shrubs.
This is forestland with a
variety of trees—oak,
hickory, chestnut, hemlock,
and pine.

Table Rock, Pickins County

Hagood Mill, just north of Pickins, had its beginnings in 1825 on land where the prominent Hagood family had a store, a tannery, and a water-powered corn mill. In earlier days ground corn was extremely important to the settlers. The mill now has a new wheel and raceway and is capable of grinding corn by waterpower.

A Hagood Mill Corn Meal Recipe Book is available, which includes recipes for Antebellum Spiced Nut Corn Bread, Bingaw's Corn Pone, Corncob Jelly, Indian Slapjack, Kentucky Corn Dodgers, Liver Mush, Scrapple, and Squash Puppies. All prove the many uses of water-ground corn.

Hagood Grist Mill, Pickens County

Along a farm road I draw a bridge, stream, road, and an old settler's cabin. It is a brisk but bright sunny day and birds are singing melodiously.   In 1775 William Bartram explored this Cherokee Indian country in the northwest corner of South Carolina. Of Keowee Village, located on the banks of Keowee River, he wrote, "Keowee is a most charming situation. . . in a fertile vale, at this season enamelled with incarnate fragrent straw- berries and blooming plants, through which the river meanders, sometimes flowing gently, but more frequently agitated,

Estatoe Community Road, Pickins County

gliding swiftly between the fruitful strawberry banks, environed at various distances by high hills and mountains, some rising boldly almost upright upon the verge of the expansive lawn, so as to overlook and shadow it, whilst others more lofty, superb, misty, and blue, majestically mount far above."

North Carolina

171 1.5

Walhalla
National Fish Hatchery
1.8

107

413

2.3

Sumter National Forest

Georgia

325

2.3

9.4

171 Presbyterian Camp Rd.

57

25

11

190

SALEM

Keowee-Toxaway State Park

Keowee-Toxaway to Stumphouse

Sumter National Forest

9.4

82

Oconee State Park

107

28

2.4

11

2.6

193

Stumphouse Tunnel

226

28

5.4

WALHALLA

28

157

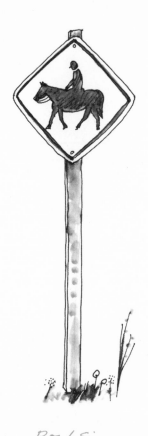

I stop at Keowee-Toxaway State Park, Upper Whitewater Falls, Oconee State Park, and Stumphouse Tunnel before reaching Walhalla. At Stumphouse a flashlight is needed to walk the long, dark, spooky tunnel, which was originally to have served as part of the Blue Ridge Railroad Line between Charleston and Cincinnati, Ohio. Work on it was begun in 1855 but, for lack of funds, the project was abandoned in 1859. If the Civil War hadn't begun soon after, perhaps the tunnel would eventually have been completed.

The tunnel has always been a popular place to visit. In horse-and-buggy days there was even a poem about it called "Let's Go to the Tunnel Today." In the 1950s Clemson University experimented with the aging of blue cheese in the cool cavern of Stumphouse.

Anderson to Abbeville

Road Sign

Pine forests, ghostly remains of old gray clapboard farmhouses, and occupied, operating farms are viewed along these back roads. I stop to draw a truly incredible array of gourd-shaped birdhouses. The air is electric with bird song. Blue martins occupy the gourds from March to August, employed by the resident Harris family to keep bothersome summer insects in check. They are later delighted to see fledgling martins just old enough to poke their heads from gourd openings. In the evenings the sky is filled with martins in flight.

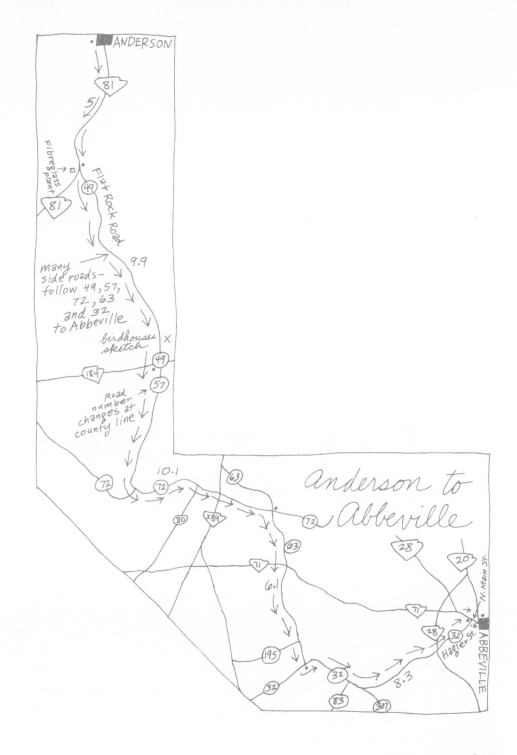

ANDERSON

81

5

Fibreglass plant

49

81

Flat Rock Road

9.9

many side roads—
follow 49, 57,
72, 63
and 32
to Abbeville

birdhouses
sketch   X

49

184   57

Road
number
changes at
county line

72   10.1   63

72

80   284

Anderson to
Abbeville

71   63

28

20

N. Main St.

6.1

71

28   32

Hagler St.

.6

ABBEVILLE

195

32

32

83   307

8.3

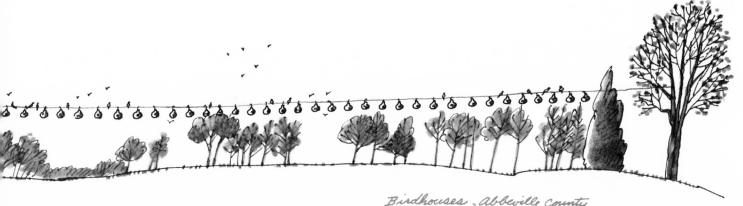

Birdhouses, Abbeville county

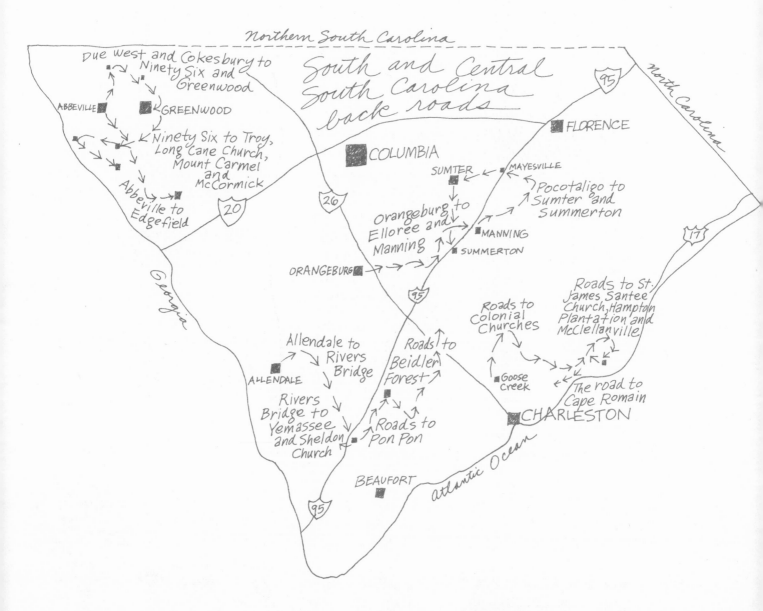

Northern South Carolina

South and Central
South Carolina
back roads

Due West and Cokesbury to
Ninety Six and
Greenwood

ABBEVILLE   GREENWOOD

Ninety Six to Troy,
Long Cane Church,
Mount Carmel
and
McCormick

Abbeville to
Edgefield

20

Georgia

26

COLUMBIA

ORANGEBURG

95

Orangeburg to
Elloree and
Manning

SUMTER   MAYESVILLE

MANNING

SUMMERTON

Pocotaligo to
Sumter and
Summerton

FLORENCE

95

North Carolina

17

Roads to St.
James Santee
Church, Hampton
Plantation and
McClellanville

Roads to
Colonial
Churches

Goose
Creek

The road to
Cape Romain

Allendale to
Rivers
Bridge

ALLENDALE

Rivers
Bridge to
Yemassee
and Sheldon
Church

Roads to
Pon Pon

Roads to
Beidler
Forest

CHARLESTON

BEAUFORT

Atlantic Ocean

95

The preservation of historic places and historic things gives me faith that South Carolina will maintain the links with its heritage for the generations to come.

John Ruskin wrote, "Watch an old building with anxious care; guard it as best you may, and at any cost, from any influence of dilapidation. Count its stones as you would jewels of a crown; set watches about it as if the gates of a besieged city; bind it together with irons when it loosens; stay it with timbers when it declines; do this tenderly, and reverently, and continually, and many a generation will still be born and pass away beneath its shadow."

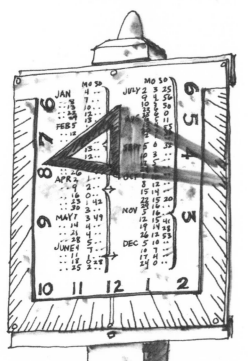

Vertical Sundial, Barnwell, Barnwell County

In Abbeville is the home of Colonel Armistad Burt where Jefferson Davis, president of the Confederacy, held the last Confederate council of war on May 2, 1865. (The home is now called the Burt-Stark House.) Davis, who had left Richmond, Virginia, after its fall, was advised by his generals to flee the oncoming United States Cavalry. Davis passed safely through South Carolina, but he was captured in Georgia on May 10.

A war memorial in Abbeville reads, "The world shall yet decide, in truth's clear far-off light / That these soldiers who wore the gray and died / With Lee, were in the right."

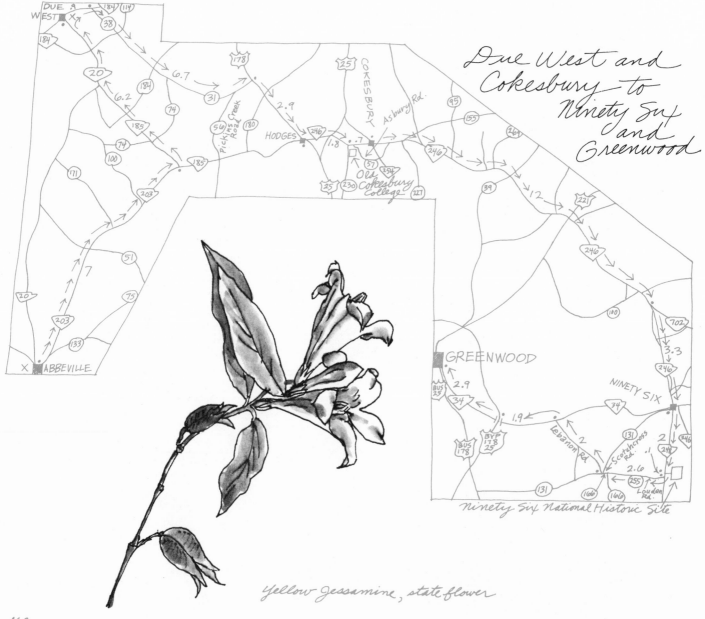

Due West and Cokesbury to Ninety Six and Greenwood

Ninety Six National Historic Site

Yellow Jessamine, state flower

Burt-Stark House, Abbeville, Abbeville County

164

Due West and Cokesbury to Ninety Six and Greenwood

As early as 1765, Dewitt's Trading Center stood where the Keowee Path crossed the Cherokee line. In 1777 a treaty between South Carolina and the Cherokee Indians was signed there. The present town, called Due West, became the home, in 1839, of Erskine College, the state's first four-year church college. In the church graveyard I draw a headstone with this inscription:

We miss thee from our home dear father
We miss you from thy place
A shadow o'er our life is cast
We miss the sunshine of thy face
We miss thy kind and willing hand
Thy fond and earnest care
Our home is dark without thee
We miss thee everywhere...
James Magill 1822-1903
Confederate Veteran 1861-1865

Back roads take me past Old Cokesbury College and on to the town of Ninety Six, once the 96th milepost on a trail used by Indian traders. It marked the distance north to Keowee Village in the foothills of the Blue Ridge mountains. The first battle of the Revolutionary War took place near here and is commemorated at Ninety Six National Historic Site where there is a pleasant interpretative trail to walk.

Associate Reformed church, Due West, Abbeville County

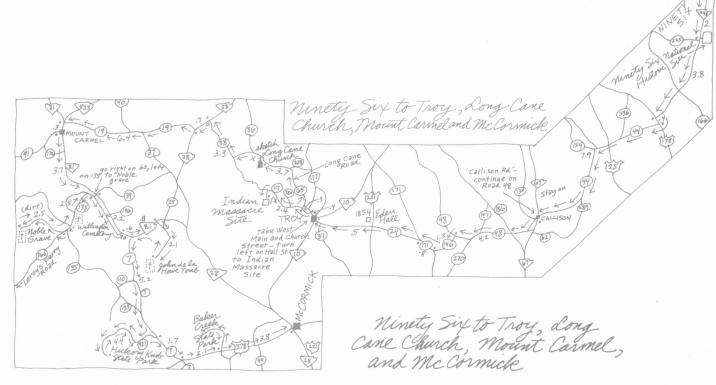

Ninety Six to Troy, Long Cane Church, Mount Carmel and McCormick

Ninety Six to Troy, Long Cane Church, Mount Carmel, and McCormick

Three miles west of Troy is the site where Indians attacked the settlers of Long Cane during the Cherokee War of 1759-61. Twenty-three victims were buried there in one grave.

In the graveyard at Long Cane Church I read this lighthearted 1811 epitaph,

In memory of Miss Jane Weir
Whose soul is fled her dust lies here
Fifty five years that's near her age,
And time she acted on this stage.
In virtues path she always trod,
And now is gone to dwell with God.

There are elegant old houses in the tranquil village of Mount Carmel.

While visiting the Noble grave site, a lovely place overlooking the big Savannah River, I sketch yellow jessamine. Its vines climb into the trees where its trumpetlike butter yellow flowers bloom profusely. This is South Carolina's state flower and its aroma is unusually delicate and sweet. My sketch is on page 162.

Long Cane Church, McCormick County

I also see the John de la Howe tomb on my day of graveyard visits. Owing to a provision in his will, one of the best examples of the virgin pine and oak forests remaining in the Piedmont area has been preserved.

At Hickory Knob I see South Carolina's only state-operated resort park.

Abbeville to Edgefield (map, page 172)

A long forest drive with little or no traffic takes me south of Abbeville toward Edgefield. I stop to see Price's Mill near Parksville, erected in 1890 after the 1888 flood had washed away the original structure. Mr. Price still grinds corn the old way, crushing it between two stones powered by water. The groan and strain of the gears is something to hear. Price says he couldn't stay in business if he had to buy electricity to run the mill!

Price's Mill, near Parksville, McCormick County

There is a large sign in Edgefield claiming it
"has had more dashing, brilliant, romantic figures,
statesmen, orators, soldiers, adventurers, and
daredevils than any other county in South
Carolina, if not any rural county of America."
This is backed up by the fact that ten state
governors have been produced from this area.
   I draw the town square facing the Edgefield
County Courthouse, designed by Robert Mills in 1839.
   Edgefield is a town of the Old South with many
grand old houses, now mellow with age, echoing times
past amid the fragrance of magnolia and honeysuckle.

On the Square, Edgefield, Edgefield County

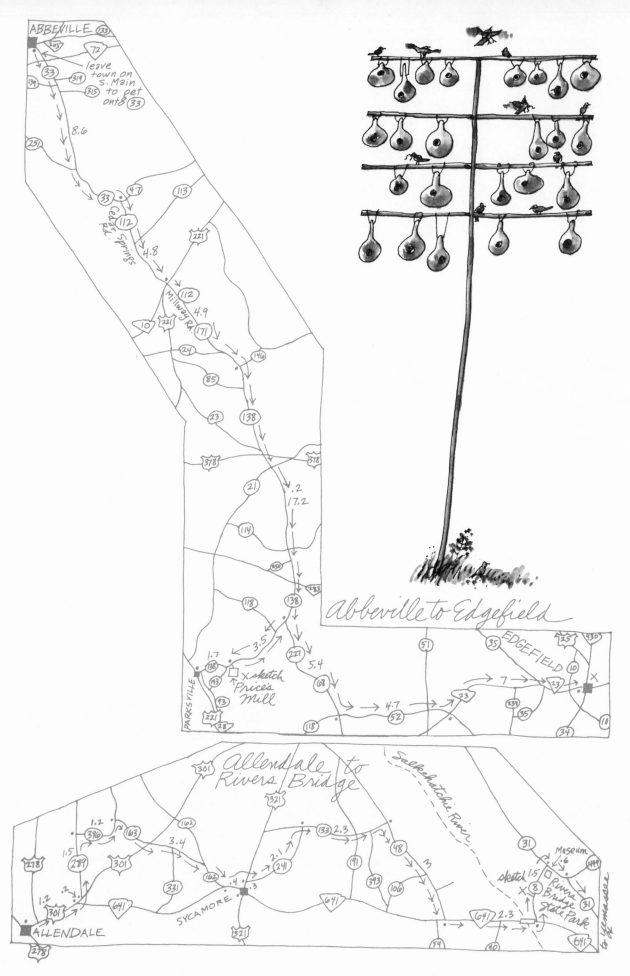

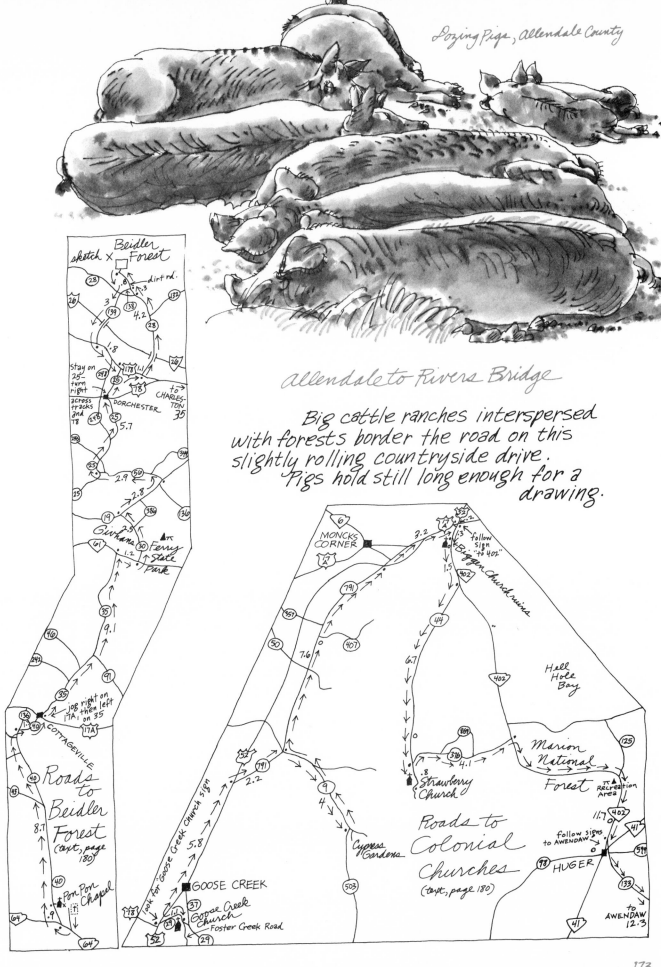

Dozing Pigs, Allendale County

Allendale to Rivers Bridge

Big cattle ranches interspersed
with forests border the road on this
slightly rolling countryside drive.
Pigs hold still long enough for a
drawing.

sketch ✗ Beidler Forest

28
dirt rd.
.8
1.3
26
3
139 138
132
4.2
28
1.8
26
stay on
25—
turn
right
248 178 1.1
35
178
across
tracks
and
78
DORCHESTER
to
CHARLES-
TON
35
248 25
5.7
246
349
25
2.9 50
2.8
19 386 136
2.5
Givhans
61 30 Ferry
State
Park
1.2
35
9.1
46
243
91
35
jog right on
17A, then left
on 35
136 40 COTTAGEVILLE
1.3
17A

Roads
to
Beidler
Forest
(text, page
180)

40
45
8.1
40
Pon Pon
Chapel
64 .9
64

look for Goose Creek church sign
52 191
2.2
5.8
78 GOOSE CREEK
1.1 37
29 Goose Creek
Church
Foster Creek Road
52
29

6
MONCKS
CORNER
7
791
851
50 407
7.6

52 A
3.2
A 1.3 follow
sign
"to 402"
1.5 402
44
6.7
402
402
Hell
Hole
Bay
869
376
4.1
.8 Strawberry
Church
Marion
National
Forest
Recreation
Area
125
11.7 402
41
follow signs
to AWENDAW
98 HUGER
599
133
9
4
Cypress
Gardens
503

Roads to
Colonial
Churches
(text, page 180)

41
to
AWENDAW
12.3

Salkehatchie Swamp, Rivers Bridge State Park, Allendale County

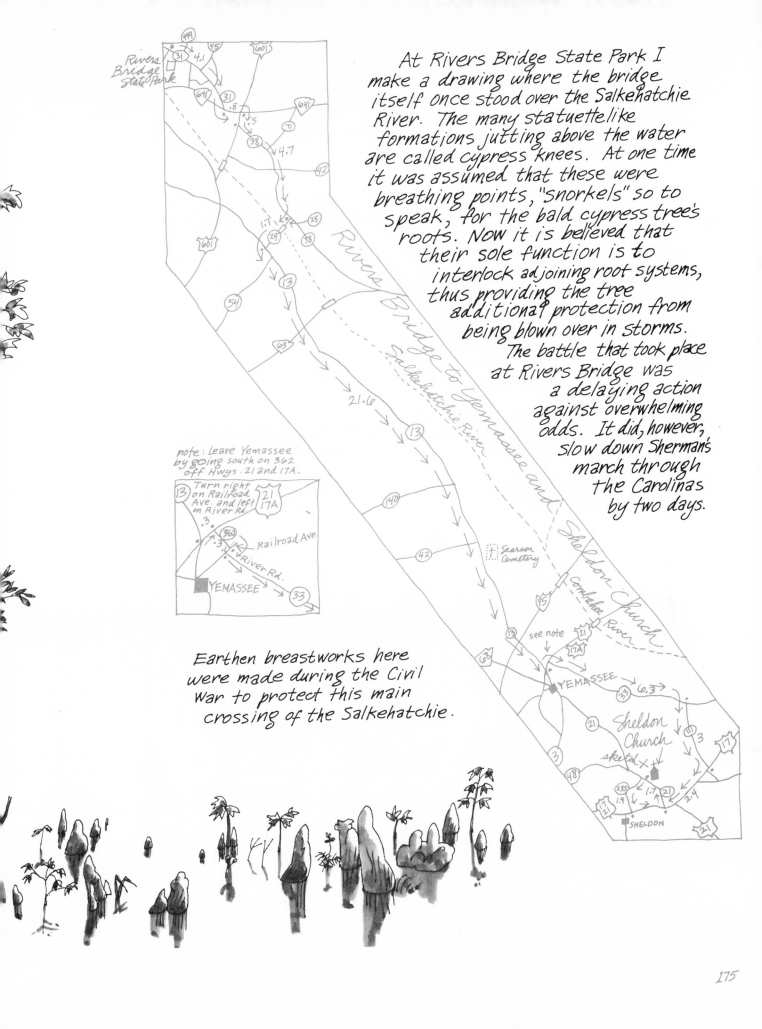

At Rivers Bridge State Park I make a drawing where the bridge itself once stood over the Salkehatchie River. The many statuettelike formations jutting above the water are called cypress knees. At one time it was assumed that these were breathing points, "snorkels" so to speak, for the bald cypress tree's roots. Now it is believed that their sole function is to interlock adjoining root systems, thus providing the tree additional protection from being blown over in storms.

The battle that took place at Rivers Bridge was a delaying action against overwhelming odds. It did, however, slow down Sherman's march through the Carolinas by two days.

Rivers Bridge State Park

Rivers Bridge to Yemassee and Sheldon Church

Salkehatchie River

note: Leave Yemassee by going south on 362 off Hwys. 21 and 17A.

Turn right on Railroad Ave. and left on River Rd.

Railroad Ave.

River Rd.

YEMASSEE

Searson Cemetery

see note

Combahee River

Sheldon Church

sketch

SHELDON

Earthen breastworks here were made during the Civil War to protect this main crossing of the Salkehatchie.

175

Sheldon Church, Beaufort County

Longleaf pine forests and farmland greet the eye along these roads. At Yemassee purple azaleas and dogwood are blooming vigorously. A three-foot-long black snake disappears from view and turtles sit stonelike on the road.

Old Sheldon's Prince William's Parish Church dates back to 1755. It was burned by the British in 1779 and rebuilt in 1826. Then the Federal army burned it in 1865. The ruins are quite beautiful in their setting of old trees and flowering dogwood.

Roads to Pon Pon

I pass a horse
hauling a man in a wagon
along these back roads,
a rare sight anywhere
in the Carolinas
these days.

In Walterboro I see
rows of fine old houses.
It is another attractive
South Carolina town.
I visit the tomb
of Revolutionary War
hero Isaac Hayne.
He was executed by
the British "contrary
to all usages of war,
August 4, 1781." There
is more to his story
for you to read
when you visit.

Pon Pon Church, Colleton County

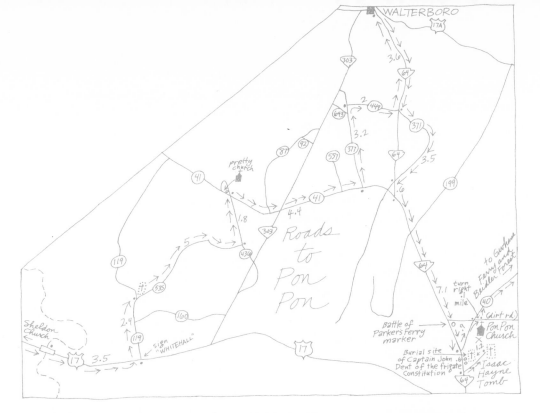

I have been searching, searching for the Chapel of Ease, St. Bartholomew's Parish, established in 1706. Finally I am directed to it by a black family who know it as the Burnt Church. It is also known as Pon Pon Church. Here I read more sentimental epitaphs. They should be recorded for they are disappearing due to erosion. Here is one:

Daniel Porteous Campbell
youngest son of Archibald and Ann Campbell
He was killed at Yemassee
In the Battle of Pocabaligo
On the 22d day of October A.D. 1862
In the 22d year of his age.
He fell in command of a section
of Company 1, 11th Regiment
of South Carolina Volunteers
With his face to the Foe,
His last words to his
Companions in arms were
Behave like Men.

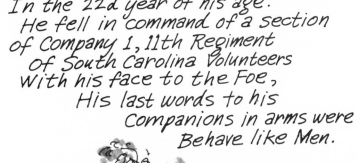

Givhans Ferry State Park is along the way to Beidler Forest. It has camping and recreational facilities.

Francis Beidler Forest in Four Holes Swamp contains the largest virgin stand of bald cypress and tupelo gum trees in the world. (The lofty cypresses may have come to be called "bald" because, unusual for their species, they lose their leaves in winter.) The tree I choose to sketch may date back to the time of Columbus, I am told. The oldest trees here are believed to be 600 years old.

Four Holes is a classic blackwater swamp fed by springs and runoff from higher surrounding areas. There is a fee to visit the museum and to walk the 1½-mile-long boardwalk. The National Audubon Society, which manages the Beidler Forest, calls the walk "A Stroll among the Giants."

Roads to colonial churches (map, page 173)

Goose Creek Church (1708) is the first stop. Mrs. E.G. Simmons, who lives next door, opens the church for me with a monster key. The interior is historic and British in feeling. George I's coat of arms hangs on the wall, and it is said that it was the presence of this royal emblem that spared the church from the British army during the Revolution. The Ten Commandments are engraved in stone near the high pulpit and a sounding board is over it. I am thrust back to early America as I stand in that richly atmospheric place.

The 1712 Biggin Church was burned twice by forest fires and once by the British. General William Moultree and Henry Laurens were among the vestrymen of the parish. The church is now a ruin surrounded by its cemetery. Here Maria Sarah Chandler and her three young children are buried. Her marker poeticizes:

Like fumes
of sacred incense
o'er the Clouds,
And wafted thence
on Angel's wings
through ways of light
to the bright
source of all (1723).

181

Strawberry Chapel is the
only building left in the early
Carolina town of Childsbury.
Situated on a bluff overlooking
Cooper River, the town thrived as
a marketplace and social center
for local planters, but by 1850
it had declined considerably.

Strawberry Chapel, Berkeley County

Wisteria climbs the massive oak, blooming purple among the limbs. A small window in the door of the church allows me to see the interior. It is a lovely, tranquil place.

At St. James I stand in the high pulpit overlooking the family boxes, re-creating in my mind a colonial congregation. The early Georgian-style church stands alone in the woods alongside a dirt road. In 1768, when it was erected, it served planters of the "French Santee" region during their September-to-March residence on their plantations.

Hampton Plantation is the ancestral home of the late Archibald Rutledge, poet laureate of South Carolina. It is now a state park. I draw the massive oak tree in the foreground that has shaded generations of families here since the earliest days of Hampton Plantation.

Hampton Plantation, Charleston County

At McClellanville I draw the "Sea Crest," a shrimp trawler whose bottom is being scraped clean of barnacles. It is but one of many colorful boats moored along Jeremy Creek in this little town of lichen-bedecked trees and old picturesque houses.

The road to Cape Romain

Cape Romain National Wildlife Refuge, 34,229 acres of land, comprises salt marshes, tidal creeks, and barrier islands. An additional 30,000 acres of open water are closed to migratory bird hunters.

At the Visitor Center I find an eastern brown pelican to draw. These birds nest on the small treeless islands in Bull Bay, as do large colonies of royal terns and smaller numbers of laughing gulls.

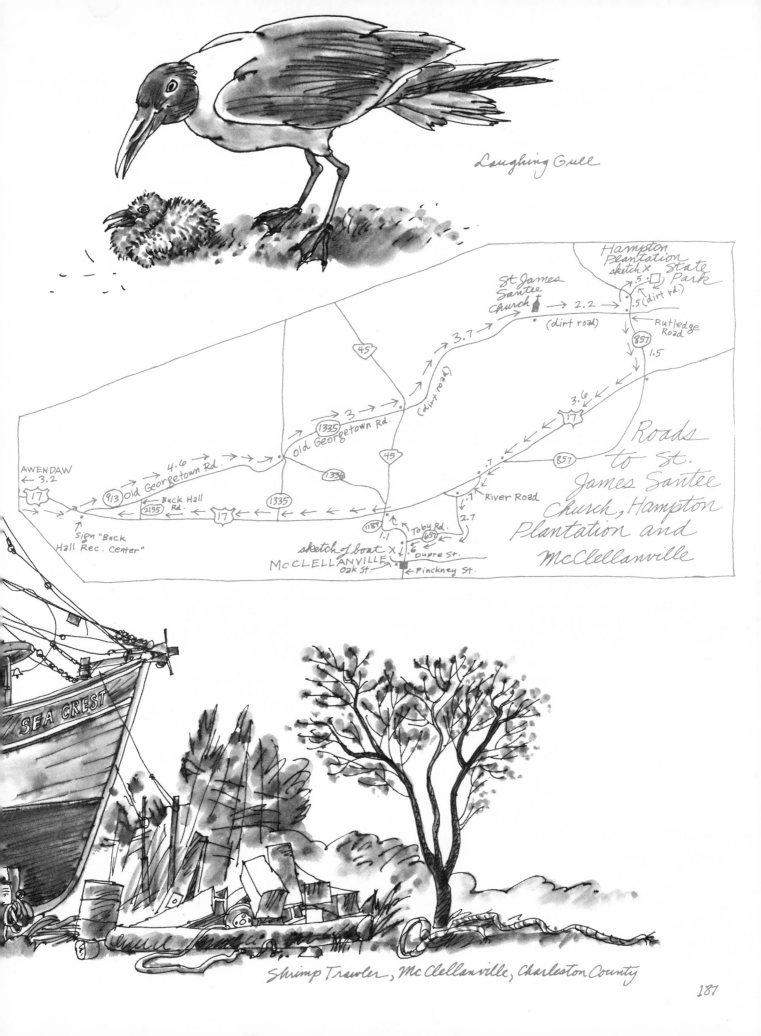

Laughing Gull

Hampton
Plantation
sketch X
State
Park
.5
.5 (dirt rd.)

St James
Santee
church → 2.2 →
(dirt road)

Rutledge
Road

857
1.5

45

3.7
(dirt road)

3.6

17

1335   3

old Georgetown Rd.

45

857

.7

Roads
to St.
James Santee
church, Hampton
Plantation and
McClellanville

AWENDAW
← 3.2

4.6
old Georgetown Rd.

1335

River Road

17
913
Buck Hall
Rd.
2155
1335
17

.7

2.7

1187
1.1

Toby Rd.
651

sketch of boat X
McCLELLANVILLE
Oak St.
.6
Dupre St.
← Pinckney St.

Sign "Buck
Hall Rec. Center"

SEA CREST

Shrimp Trawler, McClellanville, Charleston County

Loggerhead sea turtle

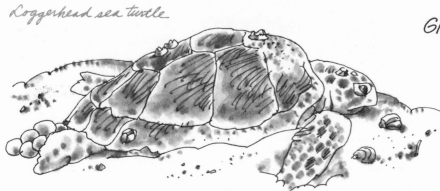

Giant loggerhead sea turtles deposit their eggs in the warm sands of the beaches on the outer islands, including Cape Island and Bull Island.

This species is 120 million years old, yet is in danger of extinction due to coastal development and the subsequent loss of nesting areas.

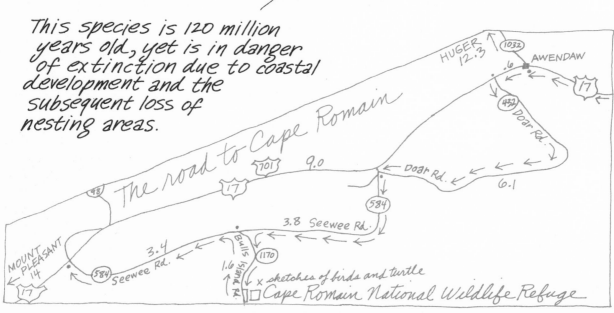

The road to Cape Romain

HUGER 12.3

1032 AWENDAW

.6 17

432 Doar Rd.

48 The road to Cape Romain 701 9.0 ← Doar Rd. 6.1

17

584

3.8 Seewee Rd.

MOUNT PLEASANT 14 3.4 Bulls Island Rd. 1170

584 Seewee Rd. 1.6

17 x sketches of birds and turtle

Cape Romain National Wildlife Refuge

Orangeburg to Elloree and Manning

Roses, wisteria, dogwood, azaleas, and crepe myrtle give color to Edisto Memorial Gardens in Orangeburg.

There is a small aquarium at the Orangeburg National Fish Hatchery where I draw a young American alligator posing with an alligator turtle. I am told that the soft-shelled turtle that was once part of the tank display disappeared one day, and the alligator is suspect.

A 10-foot alligator is in the hatchery's natural pond nearby. When sunbathing on the shore, it will let the curious get to within 12 feet of it before it slips back into the water.

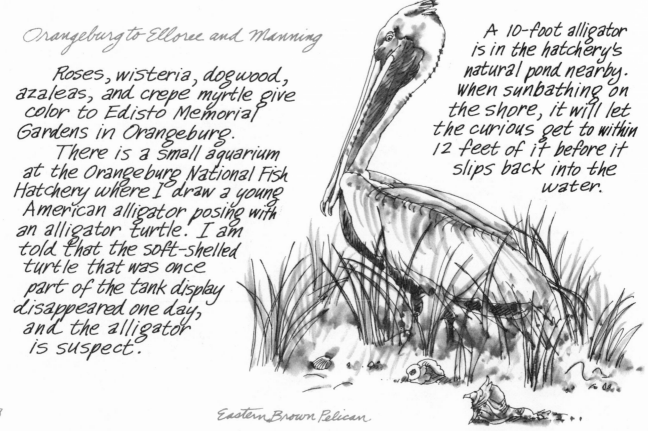

Eastern Brown Pelican

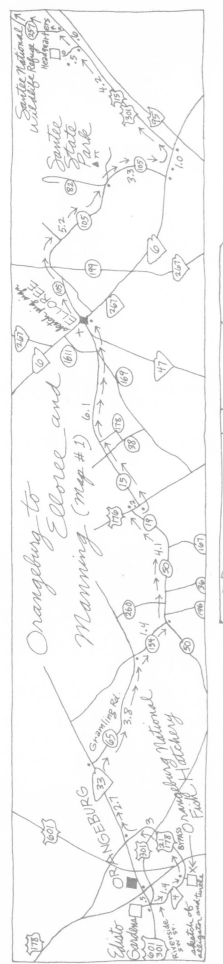

Map #1 (left panel) labels:

Santee National Wildlife Refuge Headquarters 257

Santee State Park

301 15 95

199 267 6

28 105 3.3 1.0

5.2

ELLOREE 267 267 6 611

267 47 169

6.1 178 98

15

116

Gramling Rd. 65 3.8

33 65 2.7

ORANGEBURG 301 21 178 BYPASS

Orangeburg National Fish Hatchery

260 154 50

167 136 176

154 5 50

601

1.4 1.4

601 301 Riverside Ave. 5W St. 178

Elliato Gardens

sketch of alligator and turtle

Orangeburg to Elloree and Manning (Map #1)

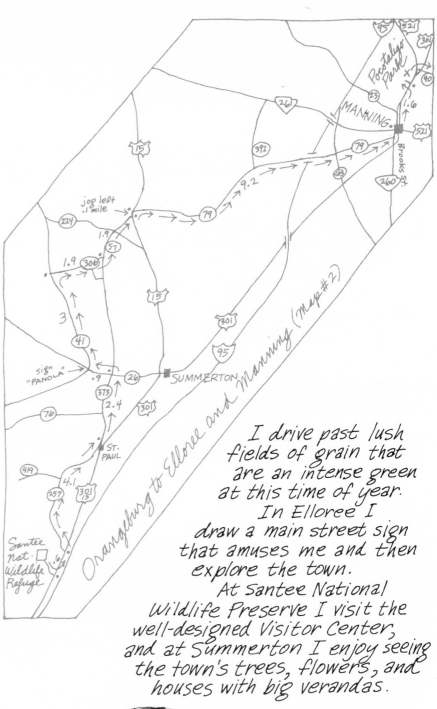

Map #2 (upper right) labels:

95 521

301

Poctaligo Park 40 1.6

23 MANNING 521

26 Brooks St.

15 392 79

79 9.2 260

224 top left .1 mile

1.9 57

1.9 300

15 301

3 95

41

sign "PANOLA" 26 SUMMERTON

.9

373

2.4 301

76 419

St. Paul

257 301 15

4.1

Santee Nat. Wildlife Refuge .6

Orangeburg to Elloree and Manning (Map #2)

I drive past lush
fields of grain that
are an intense green
at this time of year.
In Elloree I
draw a main street sign
that amuses me and then
explore the town.
At Santee National
Wildlife Preserve I visit the
well-designed Visitor Center,
and at Summerton I enjoy seeing
the town's trees, flowers, and
houses with big verandas.

Royal Tern

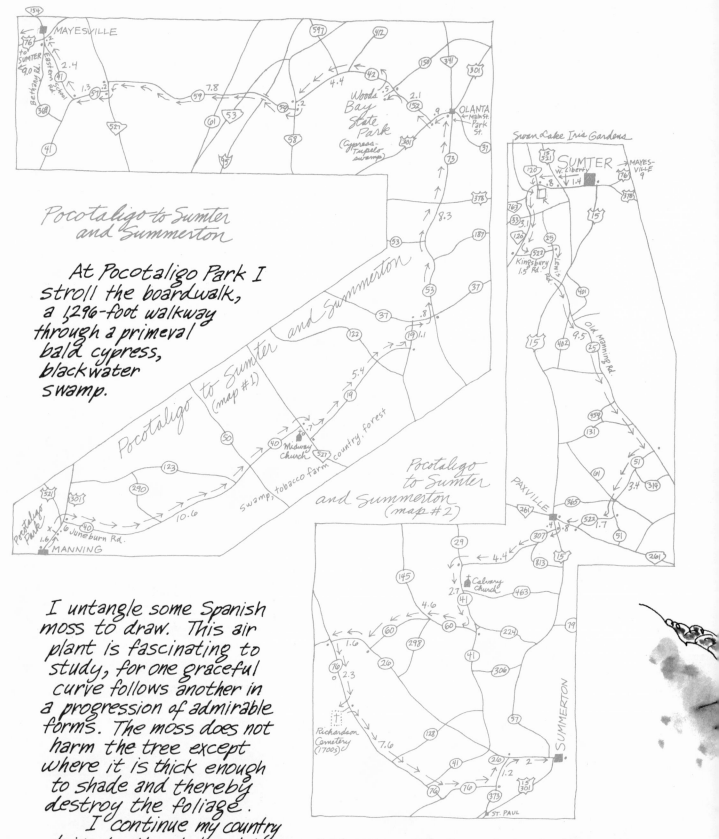

Pocotaligo to Sumter
and Summerton

At Pocotaligo Park I
stroll the boardwalk,
a 1,296-foot walkway
through a primeval
bald cypress,
blackwater
swamp.

Pocotaligo to Sumter and Summerton (map #1)

Swamp, tobacco farm country, forest

Pocotaligo to Sumter and Summerton (map #2)

I untangle some Spanish
moss to draw. This air
plant is fascinating to
study, for one graceful
curve follows another in
a progression of admirable
forms. The moss does not
harm the tree except
where it is thick enough
to shade and thereby
destroy the foliage.
   I continue my country
drive to the pleasant town of Olanta and on to Woods Bay State
Park. There is a boardwalk here through the swamp and a nature trail.
   At Mayesville I see elegant houses and big trees dripping with
Spanish moss. Mary McLeod Bethune, famous humanitarian and
educator, was born near here in 1875.

Spanish Moss,
Clarendon County.

Leaving Swan Lake Iris Gardens in Sumter, I
take the back roads to Paxville past scenic,
low rolling countryside of grainfields, farms, and forest.

Epilogue

There is a fascinating aspect to
traveling back roads over a period of
time. The strain and stress of living
in urban areas melts away. Mind and body
relax amid the charm and beauty of forest,
mountain, rural, and coastal areas. A measure
of this relaxation is the psychic shock one feels
when a major highway must be traversed or a
busy city is approached along the way.
        Let the highways and freeways speed
other travelers to their destinations. I prefer
the leisure of the back roads and hope they
always remain as they are, some simple
        dirt roads and others left unstraightened
to follow the curves and contours of the land.
        Carolina back roads I haven't yet investigated
ever beckon me to return to sample their
        unspoiled tranquility.

American alligator and
alligator Turtle

Sign in Elloree, Orangeburg county

Index

DUKES BAR BQ OPEN SAT 11-9

Book design, drawings, maps, text, and calligraphy by Earl Thollander. Anyone noticing discrepancies in maps or text or anyone aware of changes made since this book was published is encouraged to write to the author at: 19210 Highway 128, Calistoga, California 94515.